# HEALTH IN SICKNESS
# *SICKNESS IN HEALTH*

*Deep Democracy Exchange publishes books, films, music, visual art, and other forms of media that contribute to the research and development of transdisciplinary approaches to both overcome and learn from the challenges that we face as a species and as a planet.*

# Health in Sickness
# *Sickness in Health*

Towards a New Process Oriented Medicine

Pierre Morin

**Health in Sickness | Sickness in Health**
Towards a New Process Oriented Medicine

Pierre Morin, MD Ph D

Foreword by Max Schupbach Ph D

Cover design by Mediamatics

Cover photo - M.C. Escher's "Symmetry Drawing E28" © The M.C. Escher Company - Baarn - Holland. All rights reserved.

Book Design by iWigWam

Published by Deep Democracy Exchange
Florence, Oregon and San Francisco, California, USA
415-729-4333
deepdemocracyexchange.com
ddx@deepdemocracyexchange.com
Library of Congress Control Number: 2013955990

ISBN: 978-1-61971-019-1

Deep Democracy Exchange

# CONTENTS

# FOREWORD

## *by Max Schupbach Ph.D.*

Over the last few decades, many of us working in research and applications of health care have come to realize that "health" is not a measurable value fixed by science, but rather is an experiential concept in flow. It is a discussion between scientific models of biological processes, personal experiences of well-being, cultural values of what is "normal" and who defines it, political debates about public health and corporate interests, and how all of these intersect with collective identities such as gender, race, sexual orientation, and age, to name a few. Pierre Morin brings a fresh perspective into this conversation, challenging the mainstream views on health and illness. His work builds on the foundation of Processwork. In the late 80s, physicist and psychologist Arnold Mindell introduced the dreambody concept, proposing that the subjective experiences of body symptoms are symmetric to patterns found in night dreams. In short, the "unconscious" (as termed by depth psychologists Freud and Jung) expresses itself creatively in our dreams while we sleep and in our body experiences during our waking lives. Simply, Mindell stated that symptoms should not be considered only harmful, but also as potential elixirs of health and even of well-being.

This view reflected a general timespirit of that epoch, manifest as an effort towards depathologizing experiences in mental health. R. D. Laing's existential approach in psychiatry, Stan Grof's understanding of extreme states as spiritual emergencies, and Mindell's *city shadow* concept were all part of a movement away from a deficit oriented view of what is "normal."

In *Health-in-Sickness*, Pierre Morin goes one step further. He suggests that the classical approach to defining illness and health not only lacks the elixir perspective on disturbances, but in fact, also has an "opposite placebo" effect, in creating a sense of being victimized and at fault for having the symptom. His book contains many practical examples and is useful to both health practitioners as well as patients. First and foremost, it begins a long overdue conversation about the very concepts of health and sickness, and what is considered to be "normal." We are delighted to publish this book and anticipate that it will stimulate broad transdisciplinary discussions regarding individual and collective well-being.

# ACKNOWLEDGEMENTS

## *Pierre Morin*

It is Thanksgiving Day and I am on the Oregon coast in Yachats, where many of the original Lava Rock clinics were held. These clinics are the inspiration for this book. They were led by Arny and Amy Mindell and Ellen and Max Schupbach, the creative spirits behind the dreambody work which motivated me to come to the US and learn and explore this method and philosophy that looks at body symptoms as an expression of a developmental life force.

I am thankful for experiencing the spirit of creativity. It is an awesome feeling to wake up in the middle of the night with, out of nowhere, a whole outline for a new chapter.

Gary Reiss, my friend and co-author of my first book *Inside Coma* inspired me to write. His own creative abundance allowed me to believe that I could be a writer and follow my creativity.

My own ancestors were Moors and Huguenots who fled Spain and France because of religious persecution and came to Switzerland. They became doctors and public servants. As doctors, they helped the less privileged get access to Tuberculosis treatments that were previously limited to the well off. As public servants, they helped found the international committee of the Red Cross. I am grateful to my aunt Anne-Genevieve Jeanneret-Morin, who on my request researched the history of my ancestors and allowed me to connect with my own lineage. Their spirits are behind my exploration of the individual and public dimensions of health.

My uncle Pierre Girard modeled my vision of a humanistic medicine. My father, Jean-Marie Morin, with his love for the mountains and aviation, gave me the freedom to follow my own dreams. My mother, Marie-Anne Morin-Clottu, bestowed me with an interest in research and a curiosity for the world.

I would like to thank Max Schupbach, my friend, mentor and publisher for his continuous support and belief in me. It helped me overcome my doubts and take a sabbatical to write this book. We have a deep connection that, as we recently found out, extends beyond our own lives. His father was one of my grandfather's patients. After being cured, he initiated the first Tb self-help group in Switzerland. This book has elements of self-help. I hope it will inspire you to take your health into your own hands.

I am grateful to Salah Ansary, my friend and employer. He opened me to the world of refugees and immigrants, whose stories and resilience are a daily inspiration for me. Som Subedi, a Nepali Bhutanese refugee and colleague, shared with me how he is grateful every time he wakes up in the middle of the night because it gives him more time to study and catch up with the knowledge he didn't have the opportunity to learn in the refugee camp.

Many thanks to my copy editor, Raina Hassan; her sensitive corrections and feedback gave me the confidence to continue writing in my third language. My project editor, Josef Helbling, gave me much constructive feedback. Thanks to them this book improved immensely.

My wife, Kara Wilde, surrounded me with love and support. She gave me the space to spend hours in my own creative world and helped brainstorm many of the ideas that are embedded in this book.

My deepest gratitude goes to Arnold Mindell, who I met now 30 years ago in Basel, Switzerland, at a friend's gathering. Martin Vosseler was a great networker. He invited poets, politicians or anyone who inspired him to share their stories and creativity for this circle of friends. One evening, Arny came and shared his ideas and approach on working with body symptoms. I remember how he worked with Martin on a repetitive strain injury. Martin had spent the whole previous weekend folding flyers into envelopes for a political campaign. This led to the strain, or tennis elbow. Arny's creative and humorous unfolding of Martin's elbow pain piqued my interest and curiosity and led me on this path of inquiry into the dreaming world of physical symptoms, health and sickness.

Lastly, George Coppedge welcomed me on this land in Yachats many years ago. Serendipitously, we met him again this morning. He showed us the statue of Amanda De-Cuys, the Native American blind elder who was forced to walk barefoot along the Oregon coast for 80 miles in 1864, when the native people were rounded up to live in reservations. The next part of this story is synchronistic: Unaware of this story, eight years ago when he relocated, George donated this sculpture—which he had named "Amanda"—to the city of Yachats. She now stands in the middle of the forest, as school buses full of Native American children come to give her their respects and remember her story. I would like to dedicate this book to the spirit and resilience of these indigenous people and to all the individuals who, despite trauma and health problems, are seeking wellness within and beyond their sickness.

1

# *Introduction*

Writing a book about health and sickness is a difficult and complex undertaking. I won't be able to credibly cover all the many aspects this topic touches upon. What I want to do is to give my personal depiction of experiences I have had over the years working in health and express some thoughts that were inspired by my work and the many stories my clients have shared with me. This book draws upon personal accounts and experiences, the journeys and stories I was privileged to accompany and hear and theories that are based in varied fields of knowledge such as public health, psychology, neuroscience and systems theory.

As I write these lines and finish this book project, I am also participating in the latest version of health care reform in the United States. We are just one month away from implementing the Affordable Care Act, the new disputed health care law put into place by president Obama. As a result of the pressures of rising health care costs and increasing disparities in access to care, the new law aims at reducing costs, improving access to care and ameliorating the quality of care. The keywords that are associated with this so-called triple aim are: treat-to-target, hot spotting[1], evidence-based, outcomes, accountability and efficiency. The

---

1 One doctor in Camden, New Jersey, Jeffrey Brenner, used data to map "hot spots" of health care high-utilizers (one patient had gone to the hospital 113 times in a year) and found a better, cheaper way to treat these costly patients

idea is to transition from a sick-care to a true health-care model, shifting from treating the sick to preserving health and preventing sickness.

Many of the health reform strategies are interventionistic and top down. They are directed toward identifying problems and developing cures. For example, the costliest 1 percent of Medicaid[2] enrollees account for one quarter of all spending (Bush 2013). These so-called "high-utilizers" are individuals who often have addiction, mental and physical health problems and are poor. The Affordable Care Act will attempt to reduce the costs they are incurring for the whole community, and they will now be the target of huge care coordination efforts. The current linear medical model and thinking will be applied on a community-wide scale. But the problem of the few sick people that are most expensive is a problem that is nonlinear and dynamic in nature. It touches upon complex social dynamics of poverty, class, race and gender. The individual behaviors of these very sick people are intimately intertwined with the structures and relationships of our communities. Applying a pathogenic theory and mono-causal treatment approach misses the complexity of the underlying causes.

As individuals, we make health a priority and marginalize sickness. Informed by cultural values of youth, fitness and health, we make disease our enemy. We declare war against sickness and raise medical armies to fight the war and re-conquer health. There are times when we want to gather all our powers to fight against, for example, invading cancer cells. War and military metaphors might work for some people in certain precarious situations—but they inherently make disease the other, the experience that has to be fought against. This book is both a guide and a manifesto. I want to promote new ideas and a shift of our beliefs about sickness, both personally and collectively. I want to advocate for another type of health care reform, one that is not based on changing outer structures but on reforming our attitudes, beliefs and ways of relating to our bodies and their challenges. I would like us to step away from marginalizing sickness in ourselves and others and instead discover the "magic" that symptoms have. For example, my

---

through collaborative care. By better coordinating their health care, providing social services and offering house calls with nurses, Brenner's team was able to reduce hospital visits and costs by 40 to 50 percent (Gawande 2011).

2 Medicaid is the United States government's health insurance program for families and individuals with low income and resources.

asthma is a process that I want to control with my inhaler in order to breathe easier and pursue my daily activities. However, it also forces me at times to slow down, turn inward and connect with my creativity, spirit and soul. So, paradoxically, my asthma symptoms become my guide toward wholeness and help me balance my goal-oriented actions with leisure time and following my inner experiences. To my surprise, when I allow myself to follow the path of my Process, my symptoms ease. This new attitude appears to foster my own self-healing capacity. This is what I call health-in-sickness.

Let me share two more personal examples. My great grandfather Fritz Morin and my grandfather Jean Morin were the clinical directors of the Tuberculosis Sanatorium of Leysin, in the Swiss Alps. Before antibiotic treatment existed, a regimen of rest, good, clean alpine air and healthy nutrition offered the best chance that the sufferer's immune system would be able to wall off pockets of pulmonary tuberculosis (Tb) infection. Patients would spend months in these types of places, what we nowadays would call health resorts. These cures were very expensive and only accessible to the privileged. Then, during World War I and II, many men in Switzerland were drafted and spent months in confined encampments. In this environment, pulmonary Tb spread amongst soldiers and became a public health issue for the army. This led the Swiss military commission and government to have military pension and health care funds cover Tb and its treatment in sanatoriums. What had previously been a treatment for the privileged few now became accessible to active military personnel and veterans.

Many years later, I worked as a young medical doctor in the bush in Senegal. A Swiss non-profit organization employed me to help transition the local rural hospital, which had been run by Swiss doctors for many years, from a subsidized model of care to a local sustainable model of care. While the plan and intention was reasonable and well meant, it went against the interests of local community members, who didn't want to lose the privilege of foreign aid. My task was not welcomed, and I found myself standing between two fronts—the agency planners in Switzerland and the community that had welcomed me in their midst. I fell sick with malaria. I had been taking the Chloroquine malaria prevention but was infected by a drug resistant parasite strand. I had to take the stronger Lariam drug to get rid of the dangerous malaria. This drug was in its early use and the recommended dosage was highly toxic. Lariam can cause severe neuropsychiatric adverse events—in plain language, I became psychotic. I knew of the side effects and was able to understand and track my process with some awareness. During the same time I experienced this extreme state, the local population gathered together to fight against the threat of a Cholera epidemic. They marched in the streets chanting and dancing to scare the Cholera spirits away. So, here I was, lying in bed sick with malaria and psychotic, while the community chanted and danced outside my window. It was quite an intense experience, and in my mind, my individual process mixed with the community process.

Health and sickness are intricately linked with the social environment. They are complex, nonlinear processes that are both individual and communal. Tb treatment was linked to the geo-political context of that time. My malaria and Lariam-induced psychosis were connected with my bind and difficulty navigating competing needs, as well as the makeshift community rituals aimed at warding off the Cholera epidemic.

Both on an individual and community level, health has become the new standard for normality—and disease is abnormal and pathological. With my book, I would like to help shift our attitudes toward health and sickness from a pathogenic mind-set to a process- and community-based way of thinking. My hope is to foster a mind-set that sees health and disease as part of our lived experience and diversity. We need intervention and treatments to help ease suffering and pain. I want to support people to fight hard against their illness, as well as to listen to the voice of their disease and understand its message. The high-utilizers are a problem for society; however, their lives are a manifestation of social and health disparities, and we need to listen to their stories and together build renewed communities.

This book is meant for professionals, patients and the general public. As providers, you will learn to facilitate care giver-patient relationships, understand the relevance of rank and diversity in relationships, prevent burnout and help your patients and clients find a deeper understanding of their illness. As someone who suffers from disease and symptoms, you will discover tools to increase your self-healing powers and experience holistic or big health[3] that incorporates sickness. Together, we can take joint responsibility for creating a new medicine that

---

3 See definition of big health in chapter VIII.

will deliver the best possible outcomes. This book is not about specific treatment methods; it is about developing the awareness and skills to integrate psychology, social sciences and ethics into medical and mental health practice and to create good therapeutic environments and relationships. My professional journey has led me to delve into many fields of practice and inquiry. Bringing these fields together and connecting them with individual and community experiences is what I am good at and can offer the reader. After mapping the territory, we will explore the latest research and knowledge that builds the foundation for a process oriented medicine and the specific skills that help us create the best alliance possible and enhance our self-healing capacities. We then will look at the social and cultural context of health. In Appendix I at the end of the book, I include an annotated transcript of an actual individual and group-work forum to give you an idea of how I apply the concepts of a process- and community-based medicine. To help us on our collective journey into a new medicine, I also share my health-in-sickness toolkit in Appendix II, which offers a rich list of medical and experiential practices for both providers and patients. Finally, in Appendix III, I summarize the definitions I am using in this book.

Throughout the book I use different voices. One voice is interested in theory and the foundation of a new medicine (chapters III, IV and VI). Another voice is interested in the stories and lived experiences of individuals and what we can learn from them (chapters II and VIII). A third voice advocates for changes in our awareness to help build a more inclusive community and health culture (chapters V and VII). The voices intertwine and overlap. I hope to use theory to explain individual and community experiences, and I hope to draw upon all my expertise to foster in all of us a new mode of thinking about health and normality. My vision is that, together, we can achieve a new attitude that refrains from pathologizing individuals and communities and appreciates the diversity that our world is manifesting.

This book is about valuing health *and* sickness. It is about seeing sickness-in-health and health-in sickness. It is about discovering our diversity, which includes processes that go beyond the narrow margins of conventional health and normality. It's about putting an end to current conceptions of health and normality and espousing a new medical process- and community-based paradigm.

2

# *Anatomy of Health and Sickness*

In his seminal book *The Anatomy of an Illness* (1979) journalist and activist Norman Cousin describes his astonishing recovery from a severe form of arthritis using a mix of vitamin C, love, faith, hope and laughter. His book started a universal movement of self-help and self-healing using the positive powers of emotions and combating the negative effects of stress. Since then, the nature of stress and the body's ability to muster its own capacity to heal has continued to captivate professionals and lay people alike. Despite much scientific progress, health and sickness remain poorly understood. We know a lot about what causes disease and what prevents us from falling sick; nevertheless, we know little about why someone will get sick at a certain point in time while someone else with the same risk factors and exposures to the same microbe stays unscathed. At the same time, few professionals have studied the impact our beliefs and values about health have on people who are less fortunate and don't have the privilege to stay healthy. Whereas if you ask the sick, they will be able to tell you clearly how the culture of health and normality makes them sicker. This is what I call sickness-in-health.

In this chapter, I map the anatomy of health and sickness and give an overview of the body of theory that informs my thinking and practice. I am both a reformer and an advocate of the existing medical paradigms. As a child, while skiing in the Alps, I used to sing a traditional Swiss song that told the story of a mountain cottage that got destroyed by the forces of nature and then rebuilt with more beauty and strength. Interestingly enough, during World War II, both the French resistance and collaboration movements adopted the symbolic meaning of this song to foster their respective causes. This book is specific to my own journey and has a unique quality and mix of ideas. I envision that collectively we can trust Nature, with its diversity and changes, and create a new approach to health and sickness. This new way of understanding health and sickness will grow to be more resplendent, deeper and stronger.

What is health? Why talk at all about health and normality? What is normal, who is normal and who decides who isn't? What does health have to do with normality? How do we determine what is healthy? And when did we start thinking about health, or ways to stay healthy, and why?

For Carl Jung life was about self knowledge and finding one's essence or what he called the essential[4]. For him, the decisive question for mankind was: Are we related to something infinite or not? What is this essence and what does it have to do with health and normality? What are the apparent realities of health and normality and how can they guide us toward the main goal of wholeness and consciousness? I would add to that another question: if what truly matters is the infinite, how can a discussion of health and normality help us get further on the road of self-discovery?

These are some of the questions that have inspired me throughout my professional life as a medical doctor and behavioral health counselor. I worked for many years as a medical doctor and then lost my license when I moved to the US. Instead of going for my American

4 "Our unconscious existence is the real one and our conscious world a kind of illusion, an apparent reality constructed for specific purpose, like a dream which seems a reality as long as we are in it... Unconscious wholeness therefore seems to me the true spiritus rector of all biological and psychic events. Here is a principle which strives for total realization—which in man's case signifies the attainment of total consciousness. Attainment of consciousness is culture in the broadest sense, and self-knowledge is therefore the heart and essence of this process. . . . In the final analysis, we count for something only because of the essential we embody, and if we do not embody that, life is wasted." (Jung 1961, 25)

medical license I studied health psychology and Processwork[5], decided to work in behavioral health and focused on helping people overcome emotional challenges. I am a professional helper and as such have come to realize that helping has its difficulties. Helping assumes that the other who needs help is unable to help herself; it disempowers. On the other hand, we all go through times when we need professional help and someone's specific expertise to fix for example a clogged drain, someone to tell us why we have this physical or emotional pain and how to make it go away. So, what's wrong with helping and accepting help? Nothing, unless it assumes that something is wrong with you, that you are not normal, that you are excluded from other people, the mainstream, the young, healthy and fit, etc. Helping and receiving help is part of a complex process. Getting help comes with many implicit feelings of embarrassment, shyness, shame, humiliation and weakness. The relationship between the helper and the person getting the help is structured by a power dynamic. As helpers, we are in a higher-ranked position and as the person asking for help we put ourselves in a dependent position. And, as you can imagine, when our bodies' physical integrity is threatened, this dynamic is amplified a hundred times.

I have worked for many years across the cultures of medicine and psychology and learned their paradigms, languages, attitudes and implicit beliefs. Both adopt a medical or scientific, and a helping paradigm. The medical paradigm looks at causes and pathologies and wants to fix them. It is science based; it defines normal and health states based on reference values and measures the variance from these values to identify pathology, and it aims at correcting the deviation from these states or values. The helping paradigm determines who needs help from whom. It tells us that we need help from expert professionals when we move away from the health norm. It imbues us with a victim mentality when we are exposed to emotional and physical challenges. Both the medical and helping paradigm ignore the essential—the story and the meaning at the heart of our individual lives and processes. They reduce us to products of our genes and environments and omit the beauty and purpose of our particularity and uniqueness that unfail-

5 Process oriented psychology (POP), also known as Processwork, refers to a body of theory and practice developed by Arnold Mindell that encompasses a broad range of psychotherapeutic, personal growth and group-process applications.

ingly will come with disease and illness. Disease and illness are challenges that we want and need to overcome. But they are not only that. They are also expressions of our individual Process[6].

## *Health-in-Sickness*

Good and bad health are a result of multiple factors: the genes we inherited from our parents, the environment we grow up and live in, individual and community behaviors, and something I call Process[7]. The states and functions of our bodies are complex systems that are embedded in individual, community and social practices and activities. Together they inform the Process, the dynamic and directed movement in space and time, the journey that our bodies lead us through and the story that they narrate. Health is not a state but a Process and the tales and discoveries that come with health and illness are not only fateful but part of our meaningful path through life's developmental process. I hope to show that this Process is a means to discover what Jung called the essential we embody.

Let me share a personal and somewhat trivial example. For a couple of years now, both of my big toe nails have had a fungal infection. This infection is medically irrelevant and doesn't have any serious health consequences. It is mainly a cosmetic problem. Nevertheless, it is significant to me. I, at times, feel embarrassed and try to hide my toes in public when I go to a sauna or enjoy the bath in a hot tub. Why do I hide them? Who looks at my nails with judgment? What do I see that embarrasses me? The big toe nails are rougher and discolored; they are not as smooth and lean as the others. They look gross. Why do I care? I know it is medically inconsequential. On the other hand when I draw an image of how I see my nails on a piece of paper, they look like tree bark with a pattern. They actually have some character. Fungal infections are associated with uncleanliness and lack of hygiene. I'd rather have people see me as clean, gentle and friendly. What prevents me from showing my character, my roughness? I notice that I also associate this whole process with aging and the body changes that go along with aging. What makes me ashamed of my age and getting older? The

6 See definition below.

7 Throughout the book I capitalize Process when using the word in the way I explain here.

further I explore my toe nail Process the more meaning it encapsulates. It takes on this dreamlike quality.

At the same time I recall a recent interaction I had with a co-worker. This co-worker was badgering me to help her and wouldn't accept that I didn't have the time and needed to leave the office because I had another engagement. I am usually friendly, supportive and helpful but this interaction brought me out of my comfort zone and made me react more forcefully and fiercely. It brought out some of my stronger colors and character. My co-worker's unrelenting, her character, allowed me to show my temperamental toe nails.

My tree bark essence is embodied in what some would call a symptom, a fungal infection. The symptom or medical part is only one aspect of the whole dreaming process. Once explored more deeply, the toe nails remind me of part of my true or essential nature, which is more like tree bark. The medical treatment of a fungal nail infection is rough, too. You either take antibiotic pills for months or surgically excise the nail. Instead, my primary care doctor suggested I try a natural remedy. He recommended I apply tea tree oil locally. Interestingly enough, tea trees are scrubby with rough bark, which matches my Process and that part of my essential nature.

My nail Process covers many aspects, both of an individual and cultural nature: my personal growth and development of a more diverse personality with gentle and rough parts, as well as cultural perceptions of what is deemed to be normal and healthy looking and of body changes that come with age and the value we give to age. All these facets are intertwined. My toe nail Process is local and personal, as well as non-local and public, or communal.

As we see from the above personal example, body symptoms are embedded in a cultural field that shapes individual experiences. Health and sickness are rooted in a normative field that gives value and significance to some experiences and marginalizes others. What is considered normal and healthy defines the otherness of abnormal, unhealthy, bad and wrong. By using the qualifier of healthy we create the abnormality and sickness in others. In thinking that a healthy toe nail should look a certain way I contribute to the marginalization of all the toe nails that look different. Why am I so grossed out by my toe nails? Because I instinctively know that at least some people will react with some disdain, which I have internalized.

What a difference it would make if we lived in a culture that would react with excitement about the new shape and color of my toe nails and help me explore the diversity they express! How relieving it would feel if my doctor would help me uncover the essence they embody in addition to surgically removing or treating them with strong antibiotics. Many diseases and body processes are more consequential and require treatment. What I would like to offer is a conversation about ways we could do that without marginalizing the underlying Process and the person affected by the disease. Health is a state that sustains our ability to function and implement what we are here to do, to embody the essential. Paradoxically, health embraces sickness and all the experiences that come with sickness as an aspect of diversity.

One main idea I'd like to offer is that nature gives us symptoms to show us our diversity and that our uniqueness is our gift and what Jung meant by "essential." By this I mean that one function of symptoms is to reveal diversity: nature's palette of colors, shapes, fragrances and tonal qualities. Symptoms are in part an expression of our own inner complexity. They expose marginalized dimensions of our personality and identity.

Last week, I met with a client who was suffering from severe lower back pain. He has a family history of male relatives with chronic back pain. He had been moving furniture around and slowly developed an intense spasm in his back. His doctor diagnosed it as a bulging disc. A warmhearted, friendly and gentle man in his early fifties, my client had just rekindled a relationship with his estranged 22-year-old son. Three years earlier, he had conducted an intervention with his son, who was severely involved in alcohol and drugs. Because he didn't have the support of his wife, this led to a divorce and separation from his family. His son, who was 19 at the time, hired a lawyer who fought hard to force my client to pay more child support. My client experienced the court proceedings as deeply humiliating and painful. He felt harassed by a lawyer who was paid from my client's own pocketbook and who exposed details of his finances to gain more child support.

After getting together with his son my client felt relieved because his son hadn't expressed any anger or resentment. He had shared with his father that he'd had a car accident. While driving his truck, he had hit a smart car. The car had suffered no damage, but his truck had been totaled. Coincidentally, my client drives a smart car. He shared that he was planning to help his son buy a new car and that he felt he needed to be open and forgiving.

As we then proceeded to unfold the experience of his back pain he expressed the pain by making a tight fist. The fist was holding him by his buttocks and telling him to stop. As we role played the dialogue between him and his fist, the fist was telling him to be more cautious and protect himself from further emotional pain and hurt. The symptom was divulging a side of my client that he was shy to express and stand for. In a way, the back pain was an expression of my client's inner diversity.

From that vantage point health can be seen as our ability to orchestrate our own diversity dance. Health is not only about getting rid of the symptom but learning to uncover the diversity expressed in the symptom and to dance with it. For this client, health is to "dance" with his gentle and open side, as well as the side that cautions him and holds him back from being too open and unprotected. I use the metaphor of dancing to underline the fact that it is not about one or the other, being generous or being cautious, but to be able to go back and forth and have both qualities available within us.

Openness to diversity—both toward our own diversity and the difference of others—is difficult. This is why self-hatred is probably the most common disease worldwide. We feel unworthy, not good enough and are keenly attuned to what we think other people think about us. We have a list of ifs and whens, conditions and qualifications we think we need to achieve before we can feel good or okay about ourselves. *If I lose 15 pounds, when I have my master's degree, when I have a partner, when I can do this or that I will feel worthy.* We internalized the criticism we grew up with and tyrannize ourselves with high expectations and nagging self doubts. It is rare that we learned to be generous and self-compassionate with ourselves and believe that we are good enough as is. I will never forget a story that a teacher of mine told me. He was about four years old and had found his father's toolbox. Fascinated with the hammer, he was using it to beat a nail into the wooden floor of the living room. Instead of scolding him, his father sat beside him, joined him and explored with him the intriguing activity of using a hammer. He gently helped my teacher to continue on a safe piece of wood instead of the living room floor. My teacher's father demonstrated a rare, generous parental attitude and instilled in my teacher a unique sense of kindness and curiosity about the world. Most of us remember many comparable stories that include teachers, parents and other authority figures—but these stories have different outcomes. That is why practicing self-love, learning to accept our imperfections and trusting ourselves to be good enough as is, is so, so hard.

Now imagine how this plays out when we get sick or have an accident. Many of us will use the illness and accident against ourselves in the same self-hatred scheme. *God, I am so stupid, why didn't I ... I am such an idiot, I should have...* We are so accustomed to being hard on ourselves and have so much difficulty being affectionate and kind with ourselves in healthy times that it is even harder when we get sick or have an accident. Here is my point: Learning to develop a generous spirit toward ourselves and others is part of health and healing.

What goes wrong with us is part of our gift to the world, says Brené Brown in an interview on American Public Media, on vulnerability (Nov 22, 2012). Our faults and flaws are not only mistakes and errors that need correction and improvement. They are also learning opportunities and as such a contribution to the people around us; they allow us to learn from each other. In that same spirit, a way of practicing self-compassion is to be curious about our illnesses and accidents. That doesn't mean we need not be responsible, learn from our mistakes and do our best to get better and prevent similar incidents. It means we can steer away from blame and shame, to accept ourselves with our failings and learn to generously listen to the story and teaching that our bodies have to share. Be like my teacher's father toward yourself. Join in whatever happens to you with kindness, courage and open-heartedness. And for the sake of freedom and democracy don't hate yourself for being hard on yourself; allow yourself to fail in being "good," push hard until you get tired and then remember: you are good enough as is (which includes self-criticism and the desire to be perfect).

We all like to solve our health problems and stay healthy and well. However, there is another form of wellness in our ability to learn from our body's symptoms and challenges. Many years ago I witnessed how a friend with cerebral palsy discovered the "gift" that her handicap gave her. All her life she had been severely challenged by her movement and speech difficulties, confronting other people's prejudices and being treated as mentally and cognitively disabled. She had become very shy and reclusive. In a seminar I attended with her, she was encouraged to follow her own intricate movements and let them direct her. For the first time she allowed herself to give space to her particular movements, which led her to engage in a unique and ecstatic dance and connect with all the seminar participants. There is health in sickness, not only struggle.

This paradigm shift that sees health-in-sickness and values Process and diversity applies to both individuals and communities. Our individual particularities are talents that we offer to our families, friends, co-workers and communities. With our individual failings we play a part in systemic failures, which have huge implications and hurt many people. But, they are also an opening for all of us to learn together. Earlier this year, I was asked to participate in a court mandated family meeting for one of my clients. This client had been deprived of her parental right to raise her daughter after suffering a stroke and being perceived that she had neglected her child's safety. Because of her stroke my client had difficulties speaking and there were concerns that she could not attend to her daughter's developmental needs. With my input and that of other social workers, we were able to draw a different picture. Despite her difficulty speaking, my client was in our eyes a good and safe mother. The family meeting was the last step in a long proceeding of hearings and meetings. The goal was to transition the care of my client's daughter back to her mother. Significantly, both her lawyer and the child's lawyer failed to show up for the family meeting. Without them the meeting lacked the authority needed to make decisions and draft an implementable transition plan. This was one of many system failures that my client had to wrongfully endure. Despite being justifiably frustrated and angry about one more block toward getting her daughter back, my client showed incredible restraint and patience. Her speech problem had amplified her introversion and shyness, qualities that on one hand had contributed to the authorities' doubts about her ability to parent. On the other hand, her speech problems gave her a persistence and endurance that allowed her to stay resilient despite incredible challenges. Over the whole year of being separated and through the whole ordeal she became a teacher for all of us involved. Her quiet force won us all over and taught us about patience and faith. With my help she was also able to teach many people involved in all the proceedings about strokes and reverse the biases that had led people to think that someone who can't speak "normally" must be cognitively impaired, as well. In the end, everybody was caring and collaborating to draft a good transition plan.

There is unconscious wholeness in our bodies. The apparent realities of health, sickness, normality and pathology are not the whole truth. Innately, our bodies have a way to determine if something is wrong and needs to be restored. They have an inherent ability to recognize harm, to heal and to return to a previous state of better functionality. Our bodies have an inner knowledge, feedback loop and thermostat that regulate their physiologies and keep them in a state of homeostasis. In addition, they are moved toward wholeness and meaning by a life force, guiding spirit or *"spiritus rector,"* as Jung believed.

Medicine is copying nature and the inner knowledge of our bodies. With it we identify states of physiological imbalance and find ways to support the body's inner healing powers. A process oriented medicine goes a step further and facilitates self-knowledge and awareness from embodied experiences. It uses the experience of body symptoms to guide us on our journey toward the infinite and essential.

## *Sickness-in-Health*

What makes us associate health with normality? When did we begin thinking that if we didn't function well enough we were not normal? Somehow, the process of identifying harm or dysfunction to help support nature's restorative power evolved into creating categories of pathology and abnormality. Moral judgment infiltrated the discussion about health. And this led to the marginalization of diversity and created sickness as we see it currently.

Systems of morality are an attempt, says Jonathan Sacks (2000), to fight despair in the name of hope and recover human dignity by reinstating us as subjects not objects, the authors of our lives. Commonly, we are made most anxious by things outside of our control. Illness and accidents, as we know, are high on the list of concerns that are unpredictable and out of control. In contrast, moral orders create islands of personal and interpersonal meaning; they create coherence against the backdrop of uncertainty and fate. They recreate the dignity of agency and control. They free us from the blind play of external causes, such as our genome, viruses, toxins, natural disasters and so on. By applying moral notions of normality, medical systems help increase our experience of coherence and reduce our anxiety and sense of uncertainty. By dividing the world into good health and bad pathology, medicine created a system of meaning and coherence which allowed us to examine cause and effect relationships, define certain diagnosis and develop treatments and cures. At the same time, medicine relegated the experience of illness into the realm of badness and immorality. It also excluded sick, disabled and aging people from the privileges of normality and added a new level of sickness to their already challenged lives: this is what I call sickness-in-health.

The Judeo-Christian ethics of work and labor also play an important role in our understanding of health and normality. In contrast to the ethics of ancient Greece that valued scholastic endeavors over manual labor, Christian and later Protestant and Calvinist[8] ethics elevated work as a condition of human dignity. Because earning our food was perceived to be part of the creativity of the human condition, work received spiritual value. Labor elevated man, for by it he earned his food. While animals found sustenance, mankind was able to create it. Work gave humans independence and control.

Disease and illness threatens this independence, and the perceived lack of control that comes with it is stress-inducing and debilitating. Christian ethics see choice, agency and moral responsibility at the heart of the human project. With work and diligence we are not powerless in the face of fate. We can conquer disease and go back to a state of normality and health and continue our creative enterprises. This is an ideal that, unfortunately, not everybody can achieve. Illness, sickness and disability are experiences that for some will last longer, become chronic and develop into who they are. Moral conceptions of normality cast them out into the margins of society with devalued lives and challenges to their sense of self. In addition, the experience of illness and lessened ability is a daily experience for all of us, which increases as we age. Brené Brown sees vulnerability as a gift to the world and I offer an attitude toward illness that is curious about its story and meaning. Nobody wants to be ill—and I would not wish it on anyone to feel ill or to be sick or disabled. But it's an experience we all go through, more or

8 John Calvin (1509–1564) was an influential French theologian and pastor during the Protestant Reformation. He was a principal figure in the development of the system of Christian theology later called Calvinism.

less frequently, chronically and severely. After or while we fight illness and seek recovery we can learn to listen to our bodies' tales.

Health-in-sickness and sickness-in-health have both individual and collective aspects. Health and illness are both very private and extremely public. My training in public health motivates me to take a look at the social and cultural dynamics that affect people's chances to stay healthy and their experiences of health and illness. The individual's lived experience of his or her disease and disability and their course and prognosis are shaped by cultural beliefs, as well as socio-cultural systems of access to and distribution of resources and privileges. Processes of social bias, prejudice and marginalization create disease, influence treatment outcomes and have a direct impact on individuals' physiologies. Today's complex medical systems demand a change in how we perceive health and sickness. Our felt experience of bodily symptoms and diseases are predominantly influenced by social and cultural values and by the experience of environmental factors such as poverty, lack of access to education, racism, ageism and social isolation. A new view of health has to encompass the well-being of body, mind, spirit, families, communities and environments. A discussion of health cannot be solely individual.

My call for Health-in-Sickness and Sickness-in-Health is an attempt to shift our thinking and paradigm about health and illness. The new paradigm is based on process- and system-based thinking that values subjective experiences in addition to the need for objective facts, diseases and cures. In a process oriented paradigm, health and illness are subjective experiences that undergo continuous change. They are part of our daily lived experience and are rich sources of wisdom and learning. They are states that we try to achieve or avoid and processes that contribute to our diversity and humanness. A new process oriented paradigm sees value in health and independence, as well as in illness and dependence. Shared diversity and vulnerability are rich sources for community. A world of healthy and normal people is void of the wealth of human suffering and vulnerability. Again, I am not supporting suffering as a value but rather supporting the diversity of human experience as meaningful. That diversity includes health-in-sickness and sickness-in-health.

With this book I would like to help reshape the individual and community experience of health and the body beyond what is culturally normative. I would like to challenge the current mainstream notion of what it is to be healthy and able-bodied, as well as the identity politics that label people "disabled," "person of color," "queer," or "trans," and in so doing casts them to the margins of our cultures and societies. Interpersonal and community relationships are at the core of the dynamics that shape the experiences of health and normality. They nurture our beliefs and values and determine many of our behaviors, moods and attitudes. As individuals we internalize these relationships and act them out, both in self-enhancing and self-demeaning ways. They form the fabric that determines who gets accepted and who gets marginalized. Relationships are both medicine and poison.

The working alliance and relationship between health care provider and patient[9] is probably the most powerful medicine. Relationship is the "heart and soul" of medicine. There are many aspects to this therapeutic alliance. One is the narrative that the health care provider and patient create together to explain the difficulties or symptoms and the course of treatment to alleviate the problem. Another is the ritual or treatment procedure that they engage in to restore health. Narrative and ritual are possibly the most powerful tools in the medical toolkit.

The onus for creating a good working alliance lies with both the provider and patient; even so, providers have temporarily more rank or power and some added responsibility to foster an environment conducive to improvement and change. This therapeutic relationship is in many cases and situations more relevant than specific treatments. The way we align ourselves with our patients or doctors, how well we work together, is most crucial for good treatment outcomes. Medically it is relevant because it helps healing. From a process oriented point of view, relationships are magical processes in themselves that create a meaningful story and narrative between two people.

My vision is to help all of us in our roles of doctors, nurses, social workers, counselors and patients to develop the relationships that will deliver the best outcomes. Relationships are always two-way streets. They are never just influenced by one side of the relationship equation. There are power and rank issues that will affect the relationship and

9 A patient is any recipient of health care services. The word patient originally meant "one who suffers." The use of the word patient is complex and can be experienced as patronizing because it can freeze people into the role of powerless sufferer and victim. Some prefer the politically correct word of health consumer, client or individual.

give one side more responsibility (e.g., most often the provider), but we all are responsible for the relationship. As patients we can educate ourselves in ways to help create the best possible therapeutic alliance. It is in our own health interest to do that. We are responsible for taking action to prevent health problems such as quitting smoking, engaging in exercise and eating well. We are also responsible for helping create good relationships with our providers knowing that this will be the best medicine for us.

In my work as a medical doctor and now as a counselor, I was and am always interested in what works best. I intuitively knew about the importance of relationship and dialogue. Now that research demonstrates its crucial importance my intuition has been validated. In my medical studies I helped create junior Balint[10] groups for us medical students, which focused on the relationship aspects of taking a medical history and developing a good relationship. Later, I facilitated a series of Trialogues[11] between mental health providers, consumers of mental health services and their families. The facilitated discussion groups were meant to bring people together to talk about their issues with providing and receiving services. By listening to each other we empowered each participant's voice. Co-learning, learning together how to navigate the system, how to build an alliance, created community. Even though we didn't measure outcomes at this time I am sure it had an important impact on everybody's experience.

Community relationships also have the dual aspect of being either medicine or poison. High social capital[12] and community participation are linked to longevity and good health outcomes. On the other hand, we know that status and power-based community dynamics poison

---

10 The British psychoanalyst Michael Balint was a pioneer in setting up groups for medical doctors to discuss psychodynamic factors in relation to patients.

11 In Trialogue groups, users, care givers, friends and mental health workers meet regularly in an open forum that is located on 'neutral terrain'—outside any therapeutic, familial or institutional context—with the aim of discussing the experiences and consequences of mental health problems and ways forward.

12 In social sciences, social capital is the expected collective or economic benefits derived from the preferential treatment and cooperation between individuals and groups. It is based on the core idea that social networks have value.

people's health. This is why a process oriented medicine cannot avoid addressing the community aspects of health and normality. In that vein I am facilitating health equity and health leadership forums with the vision of bringing together people to share their experience, create community and find solutions for delivering what works.

3

# *Health and Normality*

*The first symptom of death is birth*[13].
Stanislaw Jerzy Lec

*Well-being is not felt, for it is the simple consciousness of living.*
Immanuel Kant

*Health is life in the silence of the organs.*
René Leriche

As we think about health and normality, it suits us to explore the origins of some of the concepts. In appendix III, I discuss in depth the definitions and roots of words and concepts I use throughout the book. In this chapter, I describe some insights from neuroscience that are relevant to our topic and then share my understanding of health, the current medical paradigm, normality, the moral aspects of normality and how these values influence our experience of health. This chapter reflects on contextual theories and ideas. If you are a more pragmatic and

13 We can rephrase the quote from Stanislaw Jerzy Lec to contend: *The first symptom is health.*

practical person I suggest you read the next chapters first and come back to this one after you have explored some concrete applications.

## *The Brain and the Mind*

At this moment in scientific development, most scientists subscribe to a materialistic view of the world, which implies that we as humans are understandable as a collection of cells, blood vessels, hormones and proteins—all following the basic laws of physics and chemistry. Some think that if we were to understand the complete physics of neurons, we would be able to elucidate the mind. Nevertheless, nobody fully understands the functioning of the brain, with its private, subjective experience of the world. The working relationship between physical matter (brain) and subjective experience (mind) is far from being solved. While we know that our mind depends on the integrity of neurons, neurons are not themselves thinking. We occupy two worlds: the world of the body and physical reality, with its material and mechanistic properties, and the world of the mind, with its cognitive properties and subjective experiences. How they interrelate is still a mystery. It would seem that the brain does not break the laws of physics, but that does not mean that detailed knowledge of all biochemical interactions will help bridge the gap. Imagine a child who finds a radio with its batteries loose. She plays with the radio and batteries and when she puts the batteries into their right place the radio starts to play music. By understanding the connection between the batteries and the functioning of the radio she hasn't yet developed a grasp on how the radio is able to transmit the music that is being played from somewhere in the distance nor what makes music so beautiful to her.

There is another gap between what our brains know and what our minds are aware of. Much of what our brain does is on auto-pilot; it happens without us being aware of it. When I play music, my brain performs multiple acts without my conscious knowledge of them. I wouldn't be able to play a tune on my saxophone if I had to consciously control the muscle activity of my fingers, the pressure on the reed and the air flow. With training and practice our brains learn and then keep knowledge of multiple activities that our minds cannot explicitly access anymore. This implicit memory system allows us to function and perform complex tasks. But as research has shown, it also informs many of our attitudes and beliefs. For example, what we call intuition or gut-feeling is an expression of our implicit knowledge.

## The Social "Nervous" System

The conscious world is an illusion and the unconscious existence is the real one, says Carl Jung in his memoir *Memories, Dreams and Reflections*. The apparent reality of the material world omits a whole spectrum of experiences. This is why a meaningful theory of human experience and biology cannot be reduced to classical physics[14] and chemistry. There are other reasons why the neural and brain pieces are not sufficient for a full understanding of human experience. Our brains are in constant communication with our endocrine and immune systems, and all three are intimately influenced by the social and material environment. The food we eat, the toxins and pollution we're exposed to and our social interactions constantly change us; and as we change, we change others. The greater nervous system, which includes the endocrine and immune system, interacts with and is shaped by the social environment. We are part of a social or non-local field: the social "nervous" system. This system has material parts that directly change us, such as toxins and germs, and non-material or experiential pieces, for example economic stress, that are as influential in affecting our physical bodies and determine our development and life course.

The social nervous system is non local and impacted by field forces[15], which means we are influenced by patterns and other nervous systems in our environment. These patterns muddle the boundaries between individual nervous systems (i.e., you and me); they are being shared in a constant stream of fluid exchanges. Our brains have the highest density of "me"-ness, but they are only the tip of the iceberg. There is a much bigger mountain and world under the surface of the water. Brains have the densest concentration of individuality and identity, but our identities expand beyond the boundaries of the brain into communications with our endocrine and immune systems and the social field and realm. The social network and environment changes your biology with every interaction, and your actions change it in return. The brain is the peak of the mountain or the tip of the iceberg—not the whole mountain

---

14 Further in this chapter we will examine how quantum physics may help bridge the experiential gap.

15 See also my discussion of field theory in chapter III.

or iceberg, which is the larger sociobiological system. The submerged mountain contains all our implicit memories and knowledge and links us with all other social nervous systems. The submerged unconscious existence is patterned by field forces and connects us with the common ground of the unconscious wholeness or Spirit, God, the Tao that can't be said, etc.

We inherit a genetic blueprint which predisposes us for certain conditions and behaviors, and then we interact with the world—which we form and are formed by. Body, mind and world are entangled and connected in numerous ways that escape our full understanding. Our experiences and identities are in constant flux: our sense of self is shaped by our biological predispositions, personal histories and involvement in the world.

### Teams of Rivals

Our brain systems and networks behave as competing teams of rivals, says David Eagleman (2011). Our brain's multiple parallel systems conflict and compete to construct a view of reality. Parts of our brains have different "values" and goals. Some are instinctual and want instant gratification and others, which are more rational, pursue long-term goals. Our mind negotiates with the different parts to create a coherent experience, narrative and explanation for that experience.

The brain is like a representative democracy with a lot of different parties, or neuronal networks, competing for power and control. The final vote of the parliament determines which party will control our actions (i.e., indulging in a craving and eating chocolate ice cream—some parts of our brains have evolved to crave the rich energy source of sugar—or to abstain from it because you are concerned about the negative consequences for your health). This example shows that two main parties dominate the debate: the rational or long-term rewards and the emotional or short-term gratification systems.

## *Multiple-World Reality*

Our brains experience the world through the lenses of multiple parallel systems and hubs of neuronal networks (e.g., emotional, rational systems, right/left brain, two different memory systems). These networks bestow more or less language-based awareness or consciousness. As a result not all experiences and memories can be verbalized. Many early childhood memories, and for example experiences under anesthesia, remain closed to a language based consciousness. These memories are processed on a neuronal level. When they get triggered they will elicit physical body reactions such as heart palpitations and sweating, or obscured feelings and moods. The various hubs include parallel simultaneous realities of, if I use myself as an example, being both gentle and engaging and strong and assertive. On some level we all share many of the possible experiences with the world. Over time, some of the experiences get marginalized, repressed or suppressed, but they might reappear under the influence of alcohol, in our dreams, in body experiences and relationship conflicts.

From a neuroscience perspective, verbally mediated consciousness is the CEO of our brain functions that steps in when automated processes, systems and routines fail, when something new and unpredictable appears that requires adjustment and adaptation. Most of our brain processes happen unconsciously, without our being aware of them. We function on auto-pilot for most of the time.

What we call personal identity is a construct of our mind that creates a unified coherent view of multiple parallel experiences. It is an ongoing process of creating a coherent narrative that explains our various perceptual, cognitive and emotional experiences. Our brains and "identities" are flexible. By processing multiple representations of the world that are accessible to us, our brains develop the neural pathways necessary for considering novel applications and expanding our identities. Thanks to the submerged world of our unconsciousness and social nervous system that contains all the alternate possibilities, realities and identities we can learn, develop new strategies and adapt to changing demands.

A multiple-world perspective allows for the existence of parallel levels of consciousness and realities. There are physical (hormonal, neuronal) and verbal levels of awareness. There is a dream consciousness and a consciousness of physical symptoms that need to be translated into the language of our CEO. One reality has health and sickness, normality and pathology as opposites. Another reality has sickness-in-health and health-in-sickness, normality-in-pathology and pathology-in-normality. One world has separate entities and experiences and another has simultaneous co-existing realities. In one world, I want to fix my problems and symptoms and in another I value them as an aspect of my diversity and particularity. In one world I am separate from you and in another I am you and you are me. In one world, symptoms and diseases are bad and wrong and in need of a cure because they hurt and cause pain. In another, they are also an experience that wakes us up to another reality; they are a meaningful gift to us and the world around us.

## Surrounding and Environing World

Our experience of the world is a construction of our brains, which produce a useful and coherent narrative of the world that is specific to each of us. It doesn't reflect the full reality of the world but only the small spectrum of the world that is accessible to us. The German biologist Jakop von Uexküll (1909) in the early twentieth century observed how various animals pick up different signals from their environment. Bats, for example, rely on a different set of signals than a tick or a knifefish, and each animal uses only a small range of possible signals. Similarly, we humans do not see or perceive the entire electromagnetic spectrum but only a narrow section of it. The animals' and our physical environment is much bigger than the individual internal experiential world. Uexküll defined the term *Umwelt* (surrounding world) for our perceived reality based on our own sensory functions and limited perceptual capacity. Uexküll's contribution lay in showing that an organism dwells in its own unique surrounding world or Umwelt. This is a world-in-itself, a unique subjective place shaped by each organism's specific mode of sensory perception.

Harrington (1999, 64) shares a biographical note of Uexküll's that describes him looking at a beech tree during a walk through the Heidelberg woods and suddenly having a thought:

> This is not a beech tree but rather my beech tree, something that I, with my sensations, have constructed in all its details. Everything I see, hear, smell or feel are not qualities that exclusively belong to the beech, but rather are characteristics of my sense organs that I project outside of myself.

In another quote Uexküll (1909, 82) states:

> Standing before a meadow covered with flowers, full of buzzing bees, darting dragonflies, grasshoppers jumping over blades

> of grass, mice scurrying and snails crawling about, we would instinctively tend to ask ourselves the question: Does the meadow present the same prospect to the eyes of all those different creatures as it does to ours?

The meadow as a metaphor describes the world outside of each organism's perceptual reality. This *Umgebung* (environing world) is the bigger reality or field that escapes our normal senses and ability to understand. We perceive only a small spectrum of the larger electromagnetic field or of our physical environment in general, and construct our own reality. We have many blind spots and very limited ways of perceiving reality. Uexküll says that each of us lives in a "soap bubble" of subjective experiences. As individuals, we experience different realities: a congenitally blind person won't experience her blindness as blackness; a synesthete[16] hears colors or tastes shapes but to her this is normal; a color-blind person doesn't miss seeing colors; everyone lives in his or her own reality or world. To function as a community, we develop a consensus and agree that my experience of red somehow matches your experience of red—even so, I might not be able to see red at all. Reality is a collectively accepted construct of multiple realities that come together to create some coherence about the joint world of experiences. Without, there would be confusion and disagreement and we would not be able to function in our everyday endeavors. Nevertheless, reality is an artificial construct that overlooks the multiple individual realities of everybody's unique experience.

Einstein says this on the first page of his book *The Meaning of Relativity* (1955, 2):

> By the aid of language different individuals can, to a certain extent, compare their experiences. Then it turns out that certain sense perceptions of different individuals correspond to each other, while for other sense perceptions no such correspondence can be established... We are accustomed to regard as real those sense perceptions which are common to different individuals, and which therefore are, in a measure, impersonal. The natural sciences, and in particular, the most fundamental of them, physics, deal with such sense perceptions.

16 A synesthete is person who experiences synesthesia or having secondary sensory experiences of for example sound as color or of color as sound.

In our everyday experience we limit ourselves to our soap bubbles and our consensus about the surrounding world (Umwelt) and its object or state-like qualities. We relegate the subjectivity of our individual experiences and the larger environing world (Umgebung) to the less fundamental worlds of myths, dreams, spirits and spirituality. Nevertheless, they are as real as the collectively accepted world of our bubbles. Mindell (2000, 27) calls the world of our bubbles, or surrounding world, *Consensus Reality* (CR) and the qualitative aspects of our individual worlds and the world outside of our common sense perception, the environing world, *Non-Consensus-Reality* (NCR). Indigenous people and shamans have always interacted in both worlds:

> The earth was composed of the physical world but also the NCR experience native people called 'Mother Earth'. In the heart of the universal human experience, we were not only independent observers but also part of an earth which itself was full of sentient beings… Favoring CR as the fundamental reality destroys the NCR sense of feeling connectedness to the world as a whole.

Throughout history, humans have engaged in many practices that allowed them to connect with the NCR or environing world. Meditation and prayer are examples of such practices. Experiments with meditating Tibetan Buddhist monks have shown a correlation between transcendental mental states and specific brain states that produce gamma waves. These electrical brain waves are of a different frequency from the electrical waves that occur during sleep or waking. These experiments show that what meditation masters have in common is the ability to put the brain into a state in which it is maximally sensitive. Besides having health benefits (stress reduction, mood elevation and increased life expectancy of the mind and its cognitive functions) these transcendental mental states produce experiences of bliss, loving compassion and a sense of connectedness.

Shamans in the Peruvian Amazon use ayahuasca, a strong herbal psychoactive concoction, to attain altered states of consciousness within specific religious rituals. People who have consumed ayahuasca report having massive spiritual revelations regarding their purpose on earth, the true nature of the universe and deep insight about how to be the best person they possibly can. In addition, it is often reported that individuals can gain access to higher spiritual dimensions. The reality that can be described in terms of our everyday perceptual bubbles marginalizes other non-consensual imaginal worlds and deep-seated sentient experiences that connect us with an essential ground, the environing world of Uexküll or what others have called Mother Nature, Yahweh, God, the Great Spirit, the Universe, etc.

Individually, we struggle with multiple parallel experiences and amongst us as people we work hard to create some sort of coherent world. We grapple with competing experiences within and between us. To survive in this multitude of possible experiences our CEO steps in and creates some unity, and as a group we create a hierarchy of experiences or a consensus reality and a hierarchy of values we call normality. In so doing we marginalize a massive amount of experiences and relegate some to the realm of difference or abnormality. When any system gives precedence to identity, a CEO or central values, it does so by defining an "us" in distinction to a "them." Individual and group identity divides and leads to tribalism and war against the stranger or the unknown. This process happens both between competing internal brain parties as well as between external groups and values. But difference does not diminish; it enlarges the sphere of human possibilities.

When we fear and fight difference and the stranger in others we do so because we constantly fight our own inner team of rivals and strangers. The challenge is not only to combat or merely tolerate the marginalized party or team in ourselves and others, but to love them as part of our own wholeness and uniqueness. Brené Brown looks at the value of our vulnerabilities and failings as part of our uniqueness, and Jung includes these in what he calls the essential. Religions have asked us: Can we see the presence of God in the face of a stranger? This begins with our own inner diversity, vulnerability and strangeness. Learning to embrace in a unifying dance the different polarities in ourselves will help us to open up to diversity in the outer world. Religions say we have to love the stranger because to her we are the stranger. On the other hand, the biggest mystery lies within ourselves and the team of rivals and strangers, the various parties of our own inner parliamentary democracy. Only then can we open up to the mystery of the outer diversity and multiple experiential realities.

## Transpersonal Psychology

Many new schools of psychotherapy reach beyond the world of consensual experiences and facts. They are based on research that demonstrates that some therapeutic outcomes are based on what individuals do internally. They help successful individuals check inside themselves for lived experiences of their situation that expand beyond the perceptual bubbles of their surrounding world. These therapies can be corralled under the umbrella of transpersonal psychotherapy. Their theories draw from the fields of humanism, existentialism, phenomenology and anthropology. They include mindfulness-based therapies, focusing-oriented therapy (Gendlin 1997), process oriented therapy (Mindell 2010) and others.

One tenet of transpersonal psychology is that we are not just related to each other and nature through the way in which we manifest externally to one another contained within the soap bubbles of our own unique perceptual worlds. We are also inwardly related to one another by virtue of sharing an inner relation to the larger meadow or environing world, which is our common ground. Drawing on phenomenology, subjective biology, quantum mechanics, process philosophy and existentialism, that larger force field is defined as a more expansive field of awareness from and within which every life form takes shape.

Through personal experience, both Gendlin and Mindell became interested in the connection between dreams and body experiences and the larger unifying forces. Gendlin, while tending to his duties aboard a ship in the Navy, realized he was pondering the "background feeling" that was left in his body from a dream he'd had the night before. He discovered that, as he continued to ponder this feeling, eventually, the whole dream came back to him. He believed the content of the dream was implicit, somehow, in the vague body-sense that was left over. This inspired his inquiry into how we as human beings can discover or rediscover information by paying attention to the subtle, embodied *intuitive feel* of our life experiences.

Mindell shares how he, as a trainee at the Jung Institute in Zurich, asked his analyst Marie Louise von Franz, one of Jung's close collaborators, why she was not able to "see" his night dreams in his momentary behaviors. She retorted that ability might be his to discover. Later Mindell treated a man with advanced stomach cancer. He asked his client to share with him how the body experience of his cancer felt. The man said it was like an explosive force coming from within, wanting to explode outwardly. While examining his experience, the man remembered a night dream he'd had of fireworks, and he also shared how he had always repressed more violent or explosive feelings. Mindell encouraged his client to express his passion, and the man went on to live beyond the time span his doctors had prognosticated. Both experiences transcend common sense realities, scientific understandings of the physical world and material cause and effect relationships.

Meditation and drug-induced altered states expand our experience of reality, as do night dreams. They convey a different kind of information and have traditionally been used in psychotherapy to examine unconscious motivations. From a neuro-scientific perspective night dreams are subconscious constructions of a narrative plot or story line that are based on a collection of experiential threads and memories. The dream narrative is less controlled and censored by the forebrain, or CEO, and thus shows a different reality or parallel world. As I describe in later chapters, many other events and experiences have similar dreamlike qualities. We suddenly get pulled into a conflict without knowingly choosing to do so, we develop a headache in a certain context even though we rarely experience headaches, we are befallen by tiredness yet we had a good night's sleep. These are examples of experiences that follow a subconscious plot or parallel reality. The cast of memories, night dreams and other "dreaming" experiences shed light on some of our subconscious self, marginalized parts of our identities and the submerged world.

If there are so many experiential realities and if most of the world is submerged and closed to conventional or consensual experiencing, is there any such thing as an objective world that is untainted by our subjective experiences, and is there anything that resembles literal truth? Our brains construe reality, and much of our thinking, behavior and remembering is "manipulated" and subjective. We are entangled with others, changed physiologically by them, and we change our environment. But then, some say "reality exists as an objective absolute—facts are facts, independent of man's feelings, wishes, hopes or fears" (Rand 1962, 35). How do we unite these two world views, the outer "objective" world with the world of subjective experiences? Our brains don't passively record reality, they actively construct it. Because we only have access to a particular view of reality, it is hard to combine the perspective of a particular person inside their world with an objective view of that same world. We have subjective experiences, such as pains and feelings, and we naturally assign them some objectivity. We believe that others have analogous experiences, even though we do not understand in the same way what they are like.

## Quantum Physics

For a possible starting point of understanding and bridging these seemingly separate worlds, we can turn to quantum physics[17]. All biological organisms must obey not only the laws of classical physics but also those of quantum mechanics. Quantum mechanics explains a range of phenomena that cannot be understood within a classical context: i.e. the fact that light or any small particle can behave like a wave or particle depending on the experimental setup (wave—particle duality); the inability to simultaneously determine, with perfect accuracy, both the position and momentum of an object (Heisenberg's uncertainty principle); and the fact that the quantum states of multiple objects, such as two coupled electrons, may be highly correlated even though the objects are spatially separated, thus violating our intuitions about locality (entanglement). Classical physics catches glimpses of the surrounding world and uses concepts from ordinary reality, such as space, time, atom and particle. In the quantum world, space, time and objects are all entangled. The precise meanings for concepts such as subject and object, specific location and separation in space, future and past are no longer valid. The patterns in the quantum world are best described by the quantum wave equation and cannot be seen or measured directly. Like the submerged world of our unconscious existence, the underground world of quantum reality escapes direct measurement.

When physicists measure quantum processes in ordinary reality, the acts of measurement and observation seem to transform quantum processes, which, without measurement, are in an infinity of possible states, into concrete physical phenomena, with real locations and velocities. And as we make that observation we disturb the final picture. This means we cannot know everything, and the physical universe can never be known independent of the observer's measurement and choices about what she observes. In addition, Einstein's relativity theory states that the forces of nature are all connected to our observational

17 For an in-depth discussion of experience and quantum physics, see: Arnold Mindell, *Quantum Mind, The Edge Between Physics and Psychology* (Portland, OR: Lao Tse Press, 2000).

frameworks, to the times and spaces of the worlds from which we observe things.

From one framework, in ordinary reality or the surrounding world, we see the world with its material properties: we measure the weight of an object; we measure the temperature of our bodies to determine if we have a fever, etc. In another framework, the quantum world, the dreamworld, the environing world, we experience the feelings of tiredness and unease that come with the fever. If you remain in the first framework your body feels like a foreign object that is dragging you down because of its fever. If, instead, you leave the objective framework, step into your inner experience of fever, and go along with the tiredness and don't resist or combat it, you will feel more at ease. What appears to be a problem from one framework is not a problem from another. I have asthma, which, at times, restricts me from breathing freely. When I go against my body and try to force air into my lungs I experience the resistance and panic. If instead, I go along with the asthma process, it pushes me into a deep inner meditative state and my breathing relaxes.

In other words, my asthma is not absolutely real as a disease. It is a problem only from an objectivistic or consensus reality (CR) framework, which defines a normal body and normal breathing in terms of weight, size, temperature and other factors. In an experiential framework my asthma is a process that connects me with my inner meditation and spiritual being. That doesn't mean I won't use my inhaler and repress the symptom to stay well, because I know the possible serious consequences of asthma. It means that I also follow my body and its "asthma" breathing and connect with my inner meditator. Whenever I take a puff of medicine I also take a minute to remind myself of the internal space my asthma wants me to relate to more.

At the quantum level, where existence of particles is determined by the presence of an observer, one is confronted with a subjectivity allowing for a new type of knowledge that transcends the material and objective world. Mindell (2000, 197) relates the indeterminacy of a quantum state, the unobserved state of a particle, to a dreamlike nonconsensual experience of reality:

> Because our normal state of consciousness marginalizes sentient, reflective processes, we become uncertain about the nature of reality... The important point is that reality rests on interactions

between the observer and the observed at levels of experience we do not always normally notice.

Based on findings from quantum physics, the physician Larry Dossey (1999) formulated a new theory of medicine that incorporates concepts of non-locality, indeterminacy and complementarity. His theory transcends materialistic views of causality. In the same way as Mindell, he applies the phenomenon of entanglement of distant particles that can exchange their quantum state with no signal involved to explain distant or non-local healing such as that of prayer circles. He uses the principle of complementarity to replace a world of mind-body dichotomies. Dossey (1999, 104) cites in his article the Indian physicist D.S. Kothari:

> The Principle of Complementarity... is perhaps the most significant and revolutionary concept of modern physics. The complementarity approach can enable people to see that seemingly irreconcilable points of view need not be contradictory. These, on deeper understanding, may be found to be complementary and mutually illuminating—the two opposing contradictory aspects being part of a "totality" seen from different perspectives.

In Alfred North Whitehead's (1966, 164) process philosophy, everything is interconnected and there are no rigid boundaries between things, thoughts, persons and events:

> ... (T)he togetherness of things involves some doctrine of mutual immanence. In some sense or other, this community of actualities of the world means that each happening is a factor in the nature of every other happening. ... [C]onsider our notion of causation. How can one event be the cause of another? In the first place no event can be wholly and solely the cause of another event. The whole antecedent world conspires to produce new occasions.

This suggestion of mutual immanence defies the materialistic prejudice of the scientific worldview. Dossey (1987, 175) advances that the idea of mutual immanence rests on modern physics and is needed to understand and treat disease and to accommodate the increasing facts that don't fit the old models of a mechanistic view of humankind.

> The ideas of Whitehead... might allow us to think of medicine in unorthodox ways: we might legitimately insert mind and

> consciousness as important factors in the world—including the world of bodies, cells, molecules, and germs;... we might begin to look seriously at the accumulating data in all medical subspecialities suggesting an important role for thought and emotion in the development of health or illness.

Dossey's ideas as well as Mindell's (1984, 2010) and Gendlin's (1997) concepts are pioneering ways to help us bridge medicine, psychology, physics and spirituality. They help us understand the unified experience of body and mind and connect them to a deeper generative force field.

The transpersonal psychology schools developed various therapeutic ways to connect to that background force field through subtle body feelings and tendencies, quick flirt-like fantasies, altered states of consciousness, a sense of feeling at home in a specific place on earth, etc.[18] By meditating on and examining these subtle experiences, we can become aware of an implicit knowledge and sense of wholeness that is based upon the force field or environing world.

## Processmind

The metaphor of the meadow outside of our perceptual senses, the quantum wave function from quantum mechanics, the force field or *processmind* from process oriented psychology (Mindell 2010) and Rupert Sheldrake's morphogenetic field (2009) describe a transpersonal process that is bigger than our individual parts. This unifying or Unitarian mind is more than our consciousness or identity. It is the experience of a transpersonal or "spiritual" state that transcends the usual experience of combating parties, energies and forces. Transpersonal psychotherapies provide many sets of practices that allow us to develop our own unique unifying dance that embraces the diversity of both our inner and outer worlds, Umwelt or surrounding world and the Umgebung or environing world.

There seem to be two parallel modes of apprehending the world. One of measuring objective data and facts and one of direct experiencing. From a process oriented perspective processes have both measurable quantitative aspects and experiential qualities. In *Quantum Mind,* Arnold Mindell (2000, 23) tells the Zen story of two monks meeting on a bridge that crosses a deep river. One monk asks the other how deep

---

18 See Toolkit in Appendix II.

the river is, to which the other monk responds by throwing him into the river.

> To know how deep the river is, you must experience its depth. … Our Zen story is deeper than that. It reveals that apprehending enlightenment means simultaneously knowing the depth of the river by using a measuring stick and by using one's own experience. … In short, we need to realize that at any moment, we live in more than one world.

Transpersonal psychology helps us build relationship between these parallel worlds. An antidote to the lack of inner coherence and distress is relationship building between the diverging fractions of our brains and minds and connecting to the environing world, or processmind.

The quantum world, dreamworld and environing world have unifying qualities. The everyday world of measurable facts and objects separates us into parts and parties. At any moment we live in a world of diversity, separation and conflicts and in a world that is "Unitarian." There is a universal truth in our shared human condition. The essential biological language is the DNA that we all share. On the level of the "meadow," where things come together, differences vanish and we are reminded of our common heritage and ground. The Sufi poet and mystic Mevlana Jelaluddin Rumi (1207-1273) said it beautifully: "Out beyond ideas of right doing and wrong doing, there is a field. I'll meet you there."

Universal processes such as economic globalization and worldwide instant communication through the Internet and the worldwide web bridge individuality and individual cultures. They transcend differences between cultures and nations. On the other hand, by negating differences and diversity they oppress the particularity of individuals, communities and cultures. A universal truth comes with the claim that it is right and the other is wrong. Any universal process or language, being faith based, economic, political, social or cultural will oppress and marginalize diversity. Democracy, for example, is the dictatorship of the majority and suppresses the minority of voters who have a different view. As I am writing these lines Barack Obama was just reelected to his second term as president of the United States. Facing difficult economic decisions, he claims a mandate of the majority who elected him to support a certain choice or direction. In so doing, he marginalizes the diversity of the public opinion, which includes alternate views about economic choices.

In a different paradigm we are the same and different. Universality and plurality go together. Jonathan Sacks (2002) says that religion is the translation of God into a particular language and culture. Arnold Mindell (2010) chose the realm of physics to describe the essential and universal dimension of the processmind. For many, processmind is God, Nature or the universal truth. Processmind then gets translated into many religions and belief systems that reflect the context of a certain time and place. Sacks goes on to describe how men tried to construct the tower of Babel, a tower that reached to the heavens and overcame the differences of language and culture. But God destroyed the tower of Babel and confused men's language so that they couldn't understand each other anymore. God created diversity and pluralism. Diversity and difference is very important; marginalization and opposing parties are needed. Paradoxically, they allow for increased awareness and understanding. The very fact that we are different means that what I lack, someone else has, and what someone else lacks, I have. Without diversity and differences, we would never need anyone else; we would be isolated and lonely, complete in ourselves. In a way the quantum world, the environing world, the submerged unconscious existence, needs the separation of the above-water world to objectify and learn about itself. Leaving the common ground and staying with our partial identities is a requirement for getting to know ourselves better.

We are all different and know what it is like to be different because each one of us has had experiences with being different, some more hurtful than others. We all know what it means to feel included or excluded, in families, work relationships, communities and social contexts. It allows us to encounter God in the face of a stranger and to recognize that "the human other is a trace of the Divine Other" (Sacks 2002, 60).

There is a divine quality to opening ourselves up to inner and outer diversity that is grounded in a common essence. We are different and the same and our differences are the playing field for learning and growth. Without diversity, we would lose awareness and consciousness. This is the dignity of difference. Biodiversity is considered a requirement for the health of our ecology. Human diversity is equally significant and something we should treasure and conserve. It is the ground for empathy and understanding on an individual and social level.

In the quantum world and because of Einstein's relativity theory, time and space are intertwined and measurable time becomes more fuzzy or variable. New research in neuroscience shows that our experience of the past is also relative and that the very act of remembering can change our memories. To build an explicit memory that lasts hours, days or years, neurons manufacture new proteins that alter the information flow across nerve synapses. Then, as we remember an event, we re-experience it in the present and create a new memory. Filing an old memory away for long-term storage after it has been recalled, the mechanism is surprisingly similar to creating it the first time. Both building a new memory and tucking away an old one involves building proteins at the synapse. When we remember, we alter the experience with the new information of the present day. The memory is re-formed in the process of calling it up. This means that memories are plastic and variable; whatever has happened since the historical event, and everything that is present around you in the environment today, changes the new memory. Our conscious or explicit memories are continuously being re-written to fit our momentary experiences and create some coherence.

One researcher stated that, paradoxically, the truest memory is the memory of an amnesiac who can't recall a memory, because his memory won't ever be altered. The malleability of memories has therapeutic implications. Alain Brunet (2008) completed a large study with nearly 70 PTSD[19] patients. He gave half the group a drug that altered their physiologic and emotional reaction to trauma while they were asked to read a script of their personal traumatic experience. Those who took the drug (propranolol, a beta blocker usually used for treating high blood pressure, sometimes for anxiety and stage fright) once a week for six weeks while reading the script of their traumatic event showed an average 50 percent reduction in standard PTSD symptoms. They had fewer nightmares and flashbacks in their daily lives long after the effects of the drug had worn off. The treatment didn't erase the patients' memories of what had happened to them; rather, it seems to have changed the quality of those memories. "Week after week the

19 Posttraumatic stress disorder (PTSD) is a severe anxiety disorder that can develop after exposure to any event that results in psychological trauma.

emotional tone of the memory seems weaker," Brunet (2008, 506) says. "They start to care less about that memory."

Immediately after the Challenger[20] explosion in 1986, the psychologist Ulric Neisser (1994) asked 106 students to describe in writing where they were when they heard, who they were with, how they felt and what their first thoughts were. Two-and-a-half years later, the same students were assembled and asked to answer the same question in writing. The new descriptions were compared with the originals. They didn't match. People had changed facts about where they were, who they were with, what they felt, what they thought. When confronted with the original essays, people were so attached to their new memories they had trouble believing their old ones. In fact, most refused to revise their memories to match the originals written at the time. What struck Neisser (1994, 61) was the response of one student: "That's my handwriting, but that's not what happened."

This form of psychological and biological editing of our memories is another way we learn from experience. We all edit our experiences to create a narrative that fits with our momentary identities and to construct a coherent system of meanings that fits our worldview and interpretation of events. When couples break up, they will usually remember their early love in another light, most probably less positive. It helps them justify the breakup. Fond memories and memories of difficult times are reframed in the light of current-day events for the sake of supporting today's sense of self. Some think that recasting old memories in the light of the present and the reconsolidation of new memories prevents us from living in the past; others that, perhaps, there is no such thing as the past. Some schools of psychology conceptualize the past and the future as marginalized experiences of the present. What we remember from the past, and what we imagine will happen in the future, are aspects of our momentary present-day process. Past and future belong to the present. Memories, present-day experiences and fantasies about the future are one lived experience and the constituents of the day-to-day and minute-to-minute Process.

Our individual worlds are a construct of particular reality-based "true" experiences and the processing of these experiences that help

---

20 The Space Shuttle Challenger disaster occurred on January 28, 1986, when it exploded 73 seconds into flight, leading to the deaths of its seven crew members.

us write a coherent narrative. Some of the editing is influenced by unconscious or subconscious motivations, which can be examined in psychotherapy. Then again, experiences, feelings and thoughts have embodied aspects and become part of our physical body experience. Psychotherapy has traditionally avoided exploring the meaning of embodied experiences and left the care of the body to medicine. Recent advances in the understanding of how stress affects the body and how certain stress reduction practices such as relaxation, mindfulness meditation, prayer and community participation mitigate stress, have opened the door to new body-centered psychotherapies. Traditional psychotherapy approaches, which are based on psychodynamic theories, see some mental and physical symptoms as an expression of neurosis. These symptoms are a compromise, expressing the conflict between a forbidden desire or impulse and a censoring and repressing force. Using a hydraulic metaphor, early theorists explained body symptoms as a result of the diversion of repressed psychic energy into the body, resulting in increased physiological arousal and strain to the body. A process oriented perspective broadens the pathological orientation, sees symptoms as part of a meaningful process, and examines feelings, thoughts, behaviors, memories, body experiences and motivations as a doorway to help us become more aware. "On this path, the important thing is neither the cure of symptoms nor the achievement of worldly goals, but awareness of the journey, step by step" (Mindell 2004, 199).

> The tao that can be told is not the eternal Tao. The name that can be named is not the eternal Name. The unnamable is the eternally real. Naming is the origin of all particular things. Free from desire, you realize the mystery. Caught in desire, you see only the manifestations. Yet mystery and manifestations arise from the same source. This source is called darkness. Darkness within darkness. The gateway to all understanding. (Tao Te Ching)

Consensus reality or the tao that can be named is only a small part of reality. The eternal Tao, the Tao that cannot be named, Jung's Unconscious Wholeness, the submerged world of the iceberg, the meadow or environing world (Umgebung), the morphogenetic field, the social nervous system, the quantum wave function are all attempts to describe parallel worlds that encompass both CR and NCR aspects. "Dreams [and body symptoms] are like maps, while the Tao that can't be said is the field guiding us through the Land through darkness" (Mindell 2013, personal communication).

## *Medical Paradigm*

Currently, medicine[21] remains in the world of the tao that can be named. It describes bodies as systems of parts that are largely independent of what the individual and health care provider are experiencing. Obviously, when we are sick and suffering, most of us want to get treatment and to restore our health and wellbeing. Medicine is here to help us understand why we are sick, to provide us with treatment recommendations and to guide us through the recovery process. Our sickness and the underlying disease become our common enemy and recovery is a version of conquering that enemy. Kay Toombs (1995, 19-20) writes of giving a speech about her experience with multiple sclerosis and being asked by audience members "to state explicitly those things that I find 'good' about my situation. Is it 'enabling' rather than 'disabling'? Has the experience caused me to 'grow' in certain ways?" To these questions Toombs answers, "Harsh though the reality may be, there is nothing intrinsically good about chronic, progressive multiple sclerosis. Nothing." Yet Toombs also writes of what she has gained through illness—empathy for others' suffering, friendships and "a clearer view of what is really important in my life" (p. 20). Most people will agree with Kay Toombs and believe there is nothing to gain from illness. There is nothing "good" about illness and no one living in even moderately good health wants to imagine ceasing to be the person they enjoy being. Among the core elements of illness are existential hardship, a threat of mind-body integrity and of personal indestructibility, a loss of connectedness, social status, of the power of rational reasoning and of a sense of control. The shock of an accident and the panic accompanying pain chase these faculties away. The experience of suffering overwhelms the patient's feelings and undermines her rational judgment. A medicine that is based in CR and focuses on the rational,

21 When I use the term medicine, I refer to mainstream Western allopathic medicine. Other complementary or alternative medical systems are rooted in different paradigms and are influencing today's thinking about medicine. Most of my arguments still apply to our general perception of medicine and the body.

factual aspects of disease and illness helps reduce anxiety and fears, assists patients in regaining a sense of control and offers great treatments and cures. But, as Arnold Mindell states and as I hope to demonstrate here, body symptoms, like dreams, can also be maps that help us navigate the world.

Medicine's CR views of disease, illness and the body are constantly shifting and incorporating older ideas from rediscovered ancient health traditions, alternative medical approaches and newer ideas often introduced by medical and scientific discoveries. The germ theory strongly influenced notions of hygiene in protecting oneself from external invaders in the 1940s. Later, the changing biomedical understanding about the role of the immune system shifted the focus from the outside to what was happening on the inside with a marked interest in nutrition, vitamins and trace minerals as immune modulating factors and agents (Martin, 1994). Only a few years ago in Switzerland, women with breast cancer explained their sickness in terms of an accident that took place several years before the occurrence of the cancer: "Sometimes in the past I hit my breast" was often heard in the women's narratives. Today, certain groups [22] in Western societies often "psychologize" cancer and other diseases, and medical processes become connected with moral behaviors. For example, there is a strong professional and lay tendency to blame people for their illness or to assign them some causal responsibility. With this attitude, cancer is related to lack of self-assertion, holding back negative emotions, repressed anger and grief and depression[23].

More recently, at the center of lay peoples' and professionals' beliefs and explanations about illness are life events and one's own lifestyle (e.g., diet and fitness). Illness and suffering are to a smaller degree seen as an essential, natural part of our lives and our mortality that comes with our natural existence, but increasingly they are considered in the sphere of influence of our responsibly lived lives. Blameworthy[24] ill-

22 Predominantly a counter-cultural group of younger, middle-class people with some interest and awareness about health issues.

23 Depression is not regularly linked with cancer, and there is no proof that one disease causes the other (Chida 2008).

24 On the other hand, I also think we don't blame ourselves enough for how we treat our physical and social environment. We self-destructively continue to pollute our bodies, our natural environment, and our relationships.

health and responsible health are the two poles of today's discussions on health matters.

This polarity manifests itself in internalized guilt-laden debates. In my work with chronically ill patients, many times individuals blame themselves for past disease-prone behaviors and self-neglect. They suffer from judgmental inner figures that reflect the larger societal debate and, to some degree, express unrealistic expectations and discriminatory attitudes. In a self-defeating reaction to the blame, they then project onto others that nobody else cares; they think they are powerless and that their individual actions won't make a difference. The blame turns into shame and hopelessness, which hinders them from acting responsibly and making healthy choices.

In the media, unexpected recovery stories receive more attention than the more frequent stories of daily struggles that yield little improvement or just delay the progression of symptoms. This cultural emphasis on success stories gives too much weight to personal achievements and too much centrality to health. The juvenile and "good-looking" body has become a symbol for a successful person. It is a metaphor for fitness and attractiveness and a standard for social acceptance and recognition. Slimness and a muscular body have evolved into central standard values and are linked to sexual appeal. The great concern in many Western cultures with faultless skin surface, deodorized youthful bodies, fit and sexy body shapes is part of a commercialized system of symbolic meanings, which aligns us with the priorities and expectations of mainstream society. Non-conforming bodies are devalued. Impaired, overweight or aging bodies are discriminated against. Old age has become a negative value and signs of aging get socially stigmatized. The body has turned into a commodity, which can be shaped and adjusted to social values. Ill, disabled, elderly or dying people are the other, those from whom the healthy and young seek, often unconsciously, to differentiate themselves. This, in turn, leads to an increasing sense of isolation and feeling of being discriminated against for people with less health privileges. The cultural, political and social conditions are left out from the discussion and life circumstances and health related behaviors are limited to individual choice and responsibility. Social processes get simplified to body events and are made treatable through discipline and control of the body. Through these embodied values, social control is internalized and political ideology materialized as corporeal feelings and physiological needs.

Many medical providers limit the scope of medicine to the factual and objective aspects that are covered by the basic biomedical sciences such as biochemistry, physiology and cell biology. They exclude the subjective or experiential aspects as well as the ethical, cultural and social issues from being part of medicine. For them, diseases are real abnormalities in the structure and/or function of molecules, cells and organs. They are real, objective and independent of subjective and cultural processes. Others see health and disease as social constructions that evolve in a specific time and social space in accordance with explicit or implicit social norms and values. Yet others see disease as natural or objective and health and healing as social or cultural or subjective.

The following story illustrates the complexities of a disease process and illness experience, as well as the entanglement of cultural and personal elements. The story is of a 60-year-old Caucasian woman of German origin who suffers from chronic bone problems and who told her story in a seminar that was held on the Oregon coast in September 2000. In her narrative, she relates her symptoms to growing up in Germany during World War II, suffering from malnutrition and getting rickets[25] disease. She still remembers hearing the sounds of the bombing resonating in her bones. She complains that she has suffered from debilitating chronic symptoms all her life and that her existence is dominated by fatigue and dizziness. She is so frustrated and fed up with being a victim that she wants to jump out of her body and leave it all behind.

The therapist, who supports her, expresses his compassion for the amount of pain and agony rooted in her historical background. Knowing of his Jewish heritage, she is deeply moved by his compassion. She states that she knows their stories could divide them and that she longs for a way to reconcile. The therapist recounts waking up remembering a song of a man on his way to the concentration camp, thinking: "Who says I have to be a calf on the way to slaughter? Why can't I be a swallow flying free?" He helps her let go of the tragedy and stay in touch with her embodied deeper self. He encourages her to leave the physical bone structure and free herself from history. A calf that knows itself also as a swallow and can live outside the finiteness of history.

---

25 Rickets is a softening of bones in children due to deficiency or impaired metabolism of vitamin D, phosphorus or calcium.

In her ongoing account she shares how in the US she lives among a community of many Jews, and how she is constantly exposed to overt and covert tensions about Germany's role in anti-Semitism and the Holocaust. This forces her to keep the story of her own immense suffering as a young child in post-war Germany buried inside, and she feels further victimized by the collective processes she endures in her community. Besides the physical pain, she experiences deep emotional and spiritual torment related to her biographical roots and collective guilt. The cause of her bone disease now includes emotional and cultural suffering. Her personal and collective histories are intricate parts of her symptom origins and actual experiences. To focus on them implies that she continues to identify with her cultural context and feelings of being a victim. With the help of the therapist she understands that her process is instead to leave the "old continent," her origins and roots behind and to "immigrate" to the new world. This would psychologically involve detaching from her identity as a German woman and from the sufferings she relates to that particular identity.

"Illness experience connects the social and cultural context and the biography of a person—not any person, but a highly specific one—to the disease process" (Kleinman and Seeman 2000, 235). The way people individually and collectively perceive and respond to health problems is shaped by the dynamics of many intertwined levels. These forces resonate and reverberate in people's bodies and thus co-create the worlds of experience and body symptoms. Illness experiences take place in the interpersonal spaces of social life and express the diversity of possible or actual ways of being in the world. They materialize under the reciprocal influence of cultural patterns of meaning, collective events and social processes, and subjective experiences.

A recent client of mine wanted to work on her weight problem. As a nurse she was keenly aware of the possible health consequences of her weight. Her experience of her weight included social judgments and rejections, somatic discomforts and worries—but also an experience of vitality, abundance and voluptuousness, which she gained by eating cake and muffins. These experiences were associated with the colors and other sensory experiences she'd had in India. Our work then centered on the individual and cultural barriers of living the voluptuous life, in addition to behavioral strategies to resist her eating addiction.

From a CR medical point of view for both the patient and the doctor something is wrong and needs a cure, fixing, help and healing. From this view there is something to restore such as health, a broken bone, abnormal sugar levels, etc. Something is out of the norm, beyond the confines of a statistical normal range or reference value. These judgments and interpretations are always based on what is considered to be the collectively accepted momentary norm, the true normal. Normal is absolute, definite, objective, continuously being adjusted and refined as our knowledge increases.

Disease and health are CR concepts that are used to define the objective and real state or condition of a person. Health and normality delineate in medicine a certain state or situation whose absence implies an illness or state of abnormality. In the last century, statistics allowed for the study of the distribution of illnesses. Reference groups of healthy people and laboratory reference values of physiological processes that were associated with health were used to define health. Medicine employed reference populations, groups, individuals and values to define health and rule out diseases. These statistical definitions marginalize the biological diversity among individuals.

Health as freedom from disease is then a state that is statistically defined as normality of function or the ability to perform all typical physiological functions with at least typical efficiency. Medical classifications require differentiation between what counts as normal (i.e., order) and what counts as abnormal (i.e., disorder). The distinction between health and pathology relies on clinical signs of physiological processes, which also define the underlying causes. These patho-physiological processes are centrally involved in the explanation, evaluation and treatment of illnesses. Some say these definitions are strictly neutral and without any personal or social values. For others, they *depend upon* personal and social values. This because health defines a person's subjective or socially constructed state or condition.

The concept of health is, as Hannah Arendt (1971, 431) said: "something like a frozen thought which thinking must unfreeze." In common sense language, we take the meaning of the word health for granted. When we speak about health, we assume a tacit understanding and consensus about the notion of health, for instance, the good and muscular shape of a healthy body or that smoking is in general bad for your health. But these CR definitions are incomplete.

Consider this story from a man with a malignant brain tumor which also illustrates the association between cancer and schizophrenia or mind and body. His experience of the tumor was of wild cancerous cells going crazy and taking over his brain. His unconventional therapist suggested he go and study crazy people in psychiatric wards and learn from them how to be "crazy," which he did. He became "crazier," and his tumor disappeared for some time.

New studies have shown reduced cancer incidence in schizophrenic and psychotic patients. One such study concluded: "The significantly decreased incidences of cancers in patients diagnosed with schizophrenia and their unaffected relatives suggest that familiar/genetic factors contributing to schizophrenia may protect against the development of cancer, especially for those cancer sites observed in both settings" (Ji 2012). From a psychological stance, one might argue that the freedom to be unconventionally "crazy" could have some cancer-protective and curative effects.

On the other hand, psychiatric patients have generally a reduced life expectancy and greater morbidity and mortality rates from cancer due to smoking, metabolic effects of psychiatric drugs, social status etc.). In the Unites States they die an average of 20 years earlier than the general population (Colton and Manderscheid 2006).

Then again, the social stress of being an immigrant is one of the critical factors in developing schizophrenia. Immigrant groups who differ the most in culture and appearance from the host country carry the highest risk. A low level of social acceptance or a high level of social rejection from the majority is linked with risk of psychotic break. Within immigrant groups individuals who feel worst about their ethnic difference have the highest risk (Selten, Cantor-Graae and Kahn 2007).

The physical and mental health picture is obviously a complex one. Biological, environmental, psychological, relational and social factors intertwine to create a process with uncertain outcomes. Classical state-oriented medical theories separate the examining doctor from her patient[26], the healthy or so called normal from the diseased and abnormal, as if they are separable from each other. They also marginalize the subjective, dreamlike illness experiences and the cultural systems in which they are embedded. The phenomenon health is so complex and elusive

---

26 For a discussion about the role of provider-patient-relationship see chapter V.

that some authors talk about the mirage of health (Dubos 1960). Others are even critical about thinking of health as a positive goal. Medieval metaphysician spoke of the *sanitas perniciosa* or *dangerous health* because good health was considered a moral risk. Health would lead to arrogance and indifference and the losing sight of the most important human endeavor, which was to seek the salvation of the soul. Today some speak of health as a privilege that come with responsibilities. When Hanna Arendt speaks of health as a frozen thought that needs unfreezing, I think of health as a Process that like an umbrella covers many fields and disciplines. A new system- and process oriented thinking and methodology is required to handle the complexity of all the factors contributing to health and disease.

Historically, individual health was perceived as the accident free functioning of organs and physiological processes, this in comparison to a well oiled machine. The more details and information we gathered about the human machine, the more complex became the understanding of its healthy working. At the same time, new statistical methods allowed for measuring the health of groups. The statistical observation of large groups allowed for identifying healthy reference cohorts and defining health based on average reference values and norms. This is how health became associated with norms and concepts of normality.

## HEALTH AND NORMALITY

Normality is linked to standardization and consensus building about units of weight and time. These trends arose with popular movements seeking more equality. During the French Revolution of 1789, a common demand of the cahiers de doléances (notebooks of grievances), was to unify weights and measures to assure that everybody was paying the same amount of feudal dues. The rallying cry: "un roi, une loi, un poids et une mesure" (one king, one law, one weight and one measure) was a slogan for more equality (Kennedy 1989, 77).

Around 1840, in England the standardization of time became relevant with the expansion of railway networks across the country. The expansion of railways required that different local times be synchronized to coordinate schedules. The times station clocks displayed were brought in line with the local time for London or "London Time." This was also the time set at Greenwich by the Royal Observatory, which was already widely known as Greenwich Mean Time (GMT).The key purpose behind introducing railway time was twofold: to overcome the confusion caused by having non-uniform local times in each town and station stop along the expanding railway network and to reduce the incidence of accidents and near misses, which were becoming more frequent as the number of train journeys increased. This is a great example of how consensus reality agreements are needed to coordinate activities, avoid chaos and suffering and promote equality and standardization.

In 1832, the German scientist Carl Friedrich Gauss strongly promoted the application of a standard metric system as a coherent system of units for the physical sciences. Gauss used this decimal system to make absolute measurements of the earth's magnetic force in terms of the three mechanical units millimeter (length), gram (mass) and second (time). Currently, the International System of Units, universally abbreviated SI (from the French Le Système International d'Unités), is the modern metric system of measurement. The SI was established in 1960 by the 11th General Conference on Weights and Measures (CGPM, Conférence Générale des Poids et Mesures). As of today, the CGPM is the international authority that ensures wide dissemination of the SI and modifies the SI as necessary to reflect the latest advances in science and technology.

As it is currently, science defines measures, which are then imposed upon the systems of society, in particular, commerce and politics. These international agreements allow scientists to speak a common language, coordinate results and develop knowledge about consensus reality aspects of the universe, the world and its parts. Normality has to do with standardization, communication and consensus building across larger groups and communities. In smaller communities individual differences play a lesser role and can be better tolerated. As soon as groups get bigger the need for concerting activities and communication becomes more relevant. These efforts tend to concentrate on practical aspects of communal living. This is why standards of measurement and notions about normality are CR concepts. Then again, according to relativity, space, matter and time are entangled and at high speeds significant distortions occur. This warping of the experiential dimensions of the universe expands our notion of reality, norms and standards and requires that we develop new ideas and ways to include the non-consensual or practical aspects.

## Moral Aspects of Health and Normality

Morality has two meanings, one that claims objectivity and one that is more subjective. In its descriptive or subjective sense, "morality" refers to personal or cultural values, codes of conduct or social mores. In this sense it does not imply objective claims of right or wrong, but only refers to that which is considered right or wrong from a specific code of ethics or morals. In its normative sense, "morality" refers to objective notions of right or wrong, which may be independent of the values or mores held by any particular community or culture.

Abiding to a factual and objective framework, the psychologist Kohlberg studied people's development of moral reasoning and identified six qualitatively different stages in a universal and invariant sequence (Kohlberg 1976). He also asserted that moral judgment is not significantly determined by socio-cultural context. But other researchers, such as Lei and Cheng (1987), found that some Chinese cultural values (the maintenance of harmony, obedience and filial piety) do affect Chinese moral judgments. Since then, other cultural factors have been found to play a role in affecting moral judgment. They are: religious values, language, cultural context, rules and expectations. Overall, though, there is now a consensus that socialization within particular cultures profoundly influences moral reasoning. This supports earlier work, which suggests that Kohlberg's stages may be neither as universal nor as invariant as had been previously assumed. Cultural context is an important consideration when assessing moral reasoning.

Within a CR medical paradigm, the term normal has, as we have seen, several meanings. At the individual organic or "machine" level disease is either present or absent, a cell is either normal or cancerous. At the community level, statistics define normality for a specific condition from its modal distribution in a population in comparison to healthy reference groups. Society defines normality by its values. Normal refers to the presence or absence of an event, a statistical prevalence (statistical normality), and to "that which is such as it should be" (normative normality). Because the degrees and boundaries of statistical and normative normality are vague and showing some continuity between the extremes of normal and abnormal, normality is often linked to cultural moral codes. The association with notions of right and wrong allows us to feel more empowered and in control and less controlled by the uncertainty of fate, microbes and natural disasters.

Hence, definitions of mental and physical health and normality show normative principles; that is, they are based on values or morals. Normality and health involve the presence or absence of illness in the biological sense, within local customs and in the subjective experience of well-being. Let us continue our exploration of health and normality and keep bearing in mind that they are associated with moral codes.[27]

The Israeli sociologist Antonovsky (1979) argues that two sharply distinguished states of normal health and ill health are insufficient for understanding how individuals and communities stay healthy. This approach cannot explain why a given individual does not break down under the ubiquity of threats to his or her health and why a given group has such a relatively low proportion of people who have broken down. He therefore postulates a continuum between a health pole and an illness pole and a conception of normality that is conceived along a continuum model. He views the final outcome of one's location on the health ease/dis-ease continuum as dependent on a long chain of phenomena that affect the individual's ability to resist ubiquitous stressors and challenges.

Dubos (1968, 67) takes a different, less idealistic approach, in his definition of health: "Health is not to be considered an ideal state of well-being achieved through the complete elimination of diseases, but as a modus vivendi enabling imperfect men to achieve a rewarding and not too painful existence while they cope with an imperfect world." This definition stresses the fact that complete health is an illusion and that the endeavor to conquer "diseases," be they related to social factors or not, solves only one part of the problem—the eradication of the causes of disease. It omits looking at how people cope with their imperfect health. He therefore raises the question of our capacities for adaptation and draws our attention to the socio-cultural and economic contexts in which this adaptation occurs.

Bartlett (2011, 233) defines mental health as "the set of typical and socially approved characteristics of affective, cognitive, and behavioral functioning, a set of characteristics derived from the reference group

27 It is also important to remember that health and normality are not only related to the health care sector, but also to security, justice, infrastructure and employment.

consisting of the majority in a society's population, and relative to which clinicians understand 'deviations from normality' and hence 'mental disorder'."

However, people perceived to be psychologically normal do a lot of bad or evil things, such as killing people in wars, destroying the environment and abusing power and rank. The classical experiments that Milgram and Zimbardo conducted in 1960 demonstrated that, providing the right context or environment, regular students were able to engage in abusive behavior. Psychological normality is linked to social conformity and validation and any normal person is vulnerable to do bad things.

Psychological health and normality are outdated concepts. We need a new Process understanding that goes beyond traditional views about normality and health. Normality as a statistical average, as adjustment and optimal functioning, as social desirability and conformity is a limiting and restrictive concept. A process oriented perspective acknowledges all conventional levels of normality and includes interpersonal and social dynamics as an aspect of global or communal learning. "I am you" or *Ubuntu*[28], the African moral code that focuses on people's allegiances and relations with each other transcends the division between normal and abnormal, psychological health and psychopathology.

Normality is defined as an individual state in comparison to a reference value and norm from a majority. I am normal, healthy or sick in comparison to a reference group. My normality is separate from the group and not defined as part of the network of the community. This perspective ignores the interdependence of and chain reactions that exist in a network of individual systems. As we will explore in later chapters, medicine, health and normality are embedded and dependent on multiple systems; some are biological in nature and others are cultural and experiential. Human biology is intrinsically linked to experience as well as social and natural environment; it is surrounded by NCR events and fields. Studies of trauma and adverse childhood events show that these have a huge impact on health. Social disparities affect health and health outcomes significantly. Values and expectations shape the course of a disease and the chances for recovery. Biology and human experience are inseparable and require a new kind of knowledge and

---

28 See also chapter V.

science that can bridge the gap between the world of objects and facts and the world of subjective and social processes, the world of physics and chemistry and the world of ethics, psychology and sociology. In my mind, medicine is the field that can lead this new translational science[29] venture.

## Health

The word "health" derives from the Old German root word "heilag" or "whole, holy." "To heal" then stands for "to make whole" and "healing" figuratively encompasses the restoration of wholeness. Healing and health are related to the concept of wholeness: physical, emotional and spiritual. Implicitly, as health care providers and "patients," we are supposed to aim toward a state of wholeness. The resulting virtue of holistic health contrasts with the fact that we are never completely whole, despite our desperate efforts to achieve wholeness by leading healthy lifestyles, eating well, exercising and engaging in therapies of all kinds. Physical and emotional symptoms are always part of our lives. Whole, unimpaired health is an illusion; symptoms are a basic aspect of our lives.

In his treatise about health and normality, Canguilhem (1989) says that being in good health means being able to fall sick and recover. Health is a process that includes sickness and recovery. Health is a feeling of assurance and resilience in life, a way of tackling existence and feeling that one is not only the owner of health but also, if necessary, the creator of meaning, values and norms. To be healthy is to feel secure in the present and assured for the future. Health is about the possibility of transcending the norm, which defines the momentary normal, and the possibility of tolerating infractions of the habitual norm (i.e., falling sick) as well as establishing new norms in new situations.

He goes on to say that health is a state of unawareness where the healthy person and her body are one. The awareness of the body consists of feeling limits, threats and challenges to health. Health depends on the possibility of it being threatened. Disease is what irritates the normal course of life or health, but without disease there is no health. Without disease we remain unaware of health; it can only be defined through the subjective experience of absence of disease. It is the indi-

29 Translational science is a cross-disciplinary scientific research that is motivated by the need for practical applications that help people.

vidual's experience within a social context that determines what for her is disease. Then, restoring health is returning to the experience of a state of health from which one has deviated. The experience of health is related to the projected past of the current illness. For Canguilhem, health is an attitude and reaction with regard to the possibility of disease. It is not an objective state or fact but an experience. Health as a collective norm does not truly exist. Today, he might say it is a process which cannot be separated from disease or illness. It is an experience that includes disease.

Like Antonovsky (1979), Canguilhem postulates there is no completely normal state, no perfect health. There exist only sick people; we are always moving back and forth on a continuum between health and sickness. Health is an individual value or a vision to which we aspire and which helps us modify our behaviors as we are sick and want to get better. Health is not a state, but a norm whose function and value is to stimulate awareness and change if threatened. As such, health is a process that includes continuous normative activity and adaptation. Canguilhem refers back to Greek medicine, in which nature, both inside man as well as outside, was considered harmony and equilibrium. To ancient Greeks the disturbance of this harmony or equilibrium was thought of as disease. On the other hand, disease was perceived as an effort on the part of nature to recreate a new equilibrium. For the Greeks, the organism develops a disease in order to get well; disease is part of the healing process to restore balance, and it is part of the solution. The imbalance comes before the disease.

Modern conceptions of health and illness are far from such an inclusive attitude. We now tend to think of health and disease in polarities. Disease now differs from a state of health and is pathological,[30] which polarizes it from the normal. The pathological is designated as departing from the normal in quality or quantity (e.g., dys- or hyper, which denotes excess, or hypo, which denotes deficiency). These qualifications exist in relation to generally accepted scales with a norm. Health then becomes the normal or norm, the preferred state. Every disease has a corresponding normal function of which it is only the disturbed, exaggerated or diminished manifestation.

30 Pathological means altered or caused by disease; indicative of disease; being such to a degree that is extreme, excessive or markedly abnormal.

In that world to be sick is to live a marginalized life. The sick individual feels different and knows how she is different. We are sick in relation to others who are healthy and in relation to our previous healthy state. Because the reference values and statistical norms or frequencies that define health express social norms and moral values, we feel excluded from the healthy when we are sick. The goal for maintaining good levels of physiological variables that are considered healthy is to promote a long and healthy life span. To accomplish this goal we need a standard definition of the good, healthy or "normal" physiological state. These physiological standards and references are determined with an average frequency and value in a given group. This norm definition omits changes and differences that occur as we age or between genders[31] and ethnic groups. The standards of good health give us an orientation and are very valuable in providing us with a direction of how to improve our health. But they skip over issues of diversity and are not value free. As such, they are also the expression of a normative social process that excludes some from the mainstream norm and, by marginalizing them, creates an additional level of sickness.

Only the "healthy" can become sick. We all know that we are healthy in a world where disease exists and we consequently know that we are susceptible to disease. We comfort ourselves with the assurance of being able to overcome sickness and disease; in the long-term we all get anxious from not being sick in a world where there are sick people. Paradoxically, we know that we are healthy not because we are stronger than the disease or stronger than others, but simply because the occasion has not presented itself yet. Illness is a test of health, and the menace of disease is one of the components of health.

Health and illness are bound together and need each other. We need the danger of illness to become aware of and learn about health. Illness is the momentary Tao of health. Challenges and difficulties or anything that "slows" us down offer opportunities to develop more awareness and consciousness, allowing us to examine who we are as individuals and groups and what our purpose is. From experiences in mountaineering, I know that the group always adjusts itself to the pace of its slowest or weakest member. That is the fate of the group. Similarly, we

31 There are sex differences in fat distribution, liver metabolism, kidney function and certain gastric enzymes. For example, women respond differently to drugs and alcohol than men.

can conceive that our individual weaknesses and illnesses are not our weakest links but our strongest ones. They are our momentary fate: they slow us down; they force us to examine ourselves and develop more awareness.

## Process oriented Health

In a process oriented paradigm, illness and health form a dance and a flow between their two separate energies and experiences. As I will elaborate in the next chapter, a symptom is an experience that challenges the status quo we call health. By exploring both experiences and their relationship to each other, we can create meaning and coherence. Together, they are an expression of our unique essence or what Jung called the essential. Every symptom is an invitation to a dance; your body is a flute being played by nature, and illness is an invitation to its essential song; they help us increase awareness of nature and life.

From a process oriented perspective of illness and health, there is a story unfolding. An aspect of disease and illness is a wake-up call to issues of our own internal diversity that we have tended to marginalize. Illness then comes to the forefront as a disturbance to help us raise our awareness about our diversity. Our identity seeks expansion; our own processmind or force field is orchestrating awareness of diversity. Seeking help, cure and relief from pain and suffering takes care of the physical body and the emotions that diseases evoke. This is only one side of the coin and overall process. Disease and illness are also helping us create meaning and coherence. The mechanical and practical aspects of our bodies' health need attention, and for some people that is sufficient and the only process. On the other hand, we can open ourselves up to the added personal development piece and use our illness experience to finding meaning and direction on our path toward individuation. From a teleological[32] point of view, nothing is wrong but a story and process unfolding in front of our eyes. A symptom is a marginalized X energy[33] that seeks attention, awakening us to an under-represented aspect of our own identity, life and story.

---

32 Teleological means that something is exhibiting or relating to some design or purpose, especially in nature.

33 X energy is everything we divorce ourselves from be it consciously or subconsciously. See also chapter III.

Advances in human genetics and proteomics (the study of proteins) are revolutionizing the idea of medical normality. These advances have enabled a more detailed understanding of individual physiological differences. What is normal for me with my metabolic characteristics might not match your normal anymore. My normal is specific to me and might differ from the group normal. The future will hold a personalized medicine that is based on a detailed understanding of physiological and biological diversity. Information about an individual's proteomic, genetic and metabolic profile will be used to tailor medical care to that individual's biological makeup and needs. The sequencing and analysis of an individual's genome (personal genomics) will allow for a personalized medicine that expands beyond the scope of group- and statistics-based normality.

Conventionally, health differs from disease and we distinguish between good and bad health. Then, as we have seen, health cannot exist without disease, and both are intertwined and depend on each other. Without occasional symptoms we wouldn't know that there is something like a state of well-being or health. Without night, day is irrelevant; without pain, you can't be pain free.

I am currently working with a young man who suffered a brain injury caused from a bike accident. He spent several months in a coma and recovered in an extraordinary way. Still, one side of his body is stiffer than the other and he presents with some cognitive and personality changes. In his own world and experience, he feels healthy and well. On the other hand, when faced with comparing himself with who he was before the accident or when others hold him up to his old self, he experiences distress. His old normal conflicts with his new normal, and his environment's notion of health, which is based on the majority's view on health, creates in him an experience of feeling unwell. Health, from his new perspective, paradoxically becomes a symptom. Cultural perceptions and definitions of health are normative. They organize our experience and the experience of our families and friends. Good health is often narrowly limited to the health we see in young, active, slender and symptom-free individuals of privileged backgrounds. From this constricted view, health excludes symptoms and so doing, it marginalizes the diversity of most people's health experiences and contributes to ill health in people like the young man I mentioned above.

A process oriented approach introduces a new dimension. The idea of following process as an aspect of nature's manifestation allows us to stay with a person's experience and the many contextual factors that shape the experience. We see the old and new normal and the dynamics between them. We can appreciate the wellness that exists in sickness and the struggle to fit with a mainstream expectation of good health. Health and normality create a division between those of us who are healthy, normal and well in conventional ways and those who have a different health—not a disease or disability, but a different ease and a different ability.

"Health" defines ideal behaviors and experiences. The new normal of the disease experience are evaluated within a framework of a previous state of health and not as a process. Previous perceived normal behaviors and experiences are compared with new experiences. This relationship between internal and external preferred experiences is what contributes to the feelings of being sick and different. As a Process, new experiences are taken as such without bias or partiality. The social definition of preferred experiences or health adds another layer of illness to the experience of disease. With impartiality, disease and illness are new dimensions of life. From a process oriented understanding, there is no disorder—only the substitution of a preferred order with another. The mainstream normative process amplifies suffering, but a process oriented way creates no difference or pain.

There are many definitions of health, and all shed light on important aspects of it. Some stress the biological and material causes that endanger health, some look at the social and cultural context of health and others identify the positive aspects of the illness experience. Health, in its "universal" normative nature, is needed as a guide post. But it also marginalizes individual differences and diversity. A process oriented individual definition of health sees health as a somatic feeling connection to one's deepest self. That life force or force field (processmind) is the maker of dreams and the inner compass that points us toward our next step. On a community level, health is our collective ability to engage all the voices and facilitate the relationship between them.

4

# *A Process oriented Medicine*

As we have explored in chapter III, health is not a state but a process that is guided by a norm or standard and which, when threatened, stimulates our awareness and motivates us to change. In this chapter I discuss the theories that lay the foundation for a process oriented medicine. I illustrate them with examples and stories and go over some of the Processwork methods.

Health is a vision or dream and as such it creates a directional and motivational pull for us to overcome our health challenges and injuries. Without this vision there is no reason for change and improvement. Health is an aspect of our life force and drive that motivates us to get up in the morning and step onto the treadmill; go for our daily 30-minute walk; avoid coffee, alcohol and nicotine; and eat our greens.

Paradoxically, we wouldn't be motivated to change, stay healthy or get well if we didn't experience any threat to our health or well-being. Our fatigues, aches and pains, our anxieties and low moods, the difficulties we encounter in our jobs and relationships—they are all educational and growing opportunities, without which we would not change, learn and develop more awareness. Athletes learn from their hamstring injury to adjust their pace and training and correct their technique. Employees learn from conflict with their co-worker to improve their teamwork skills. Without symptoms, injuries and challenges, we remain unaware of learning and growth opportunities. There is health in sickness and healing; thus is the change and improvement we make based on the perceived or experienced threat to our personal vision of good health. Without movement or change there is no health, and without injuries or challenges we wouldn't be motivated to change.

Process means to move forward. Nature and life are in constant motion and change. Stillness and feeling stuck are an illusion. But why is it that we feel hopeless when we are depressed, and why is it that we can't see change when we feel low and sick? We are used to thinking in terms of certain states and parts. We are sick or well, we feel hopeful or depressed, we are normal or crazy, we are sensitive or unconcerned. We confine ourselves and others in time and space to certain states, identities and behaviors. A part- and state-oriented thinking allows us to analyze our thinking, behaviors, relationships, world events and health issues. We can evaluate and identify problems, what causes what and who is responsible for doing what to whom. Our mind and body states are separate from each other, and we are separate individual selves responsible for our own individual actions. A process oriented perspective focuses on the flow and movement between states and the overall patterns, rather than individual details. From this view, the Process manifests itself in and flows between body, emotional and relationship problems. Processes and patterns have their own intelligence and meaning and cannot be reduced to the individual part-like states. Process is the inalienable power of life force, the élan vital (Bergson 1911) that keeps us getting up in the morning despite sadness, despair, worries and anxiety.

The details and parts are relevant; they need attention and help us find solutions and cures. From a process oriented perspective, individual states and facts are expressions of a path and direction. They are interconnected and influence each other's paths. In a state orientation we seek, through psychotherapy and medicine, relief from sickness and distress and look for positive outcomes, health and emotional wellness. From a process angle we are whole no matter what, a manifestation of a path, entwined with the paths of others, in a web of forces that remain a mystery, whose exact nature can never be fully known. Our bodies' problems, our relationship, cultural and environmental problems, are expressions of that path and help us become aware of the diversity issues and the common ground we share. They are necessary for all of us to learn and grow. The larger process view integrates and appreciates state- and parts-oriented thinking, as they help us recognize differences, individual and cultural nuances, and the uniqueness of personal and general history.

I view change as healing and healing as change. Except nature doesn't always produce the outcomes we want and hope for. A process perspective allows us to embrace the ongoing flow of nature, which in my view includes the cultural forces that inform the field of psychotherapy and medicine. Our social environments inform our everyday practice and the expectations of our clients and their families. A process oriented approach facilitates the dynamics of the client's social environment and her ability to reveal and believe in the inherent intelligence of her experience. Not everybody will be able to or should trust in the paradox of the self-healing powers of sickness, feeling stuck and hopelessness.

Jung and Freud believed the "royal road to the unconscious is through dreams." For newer psychotherapeutic schools, that road is not the only one[34]. There are other ways into the unconscious, such as body experiences, unintentional body movements, relationship processes, comatose states and large-group interactions.

As we have seen, dreams are subconscious constructions of a narrative plot or story line from a collection of experiential threads and memories. The dream narrative is less controlled and censored by our brain's CEO, the forebrain, and thus shows a different reality or parallel world[35]. Dreams take us to experiential worlds that are outside social norms and far from consensus reality. In this world our inalienable process shows itself in new clothes. We are not bound to our socially conformist identity and are free to experience new parallel worlds[36]. While our brains process multiple realities at the same time, some remain unconscious while others receive the privilege of our consciousness. Some psychological treatments examine the subconscious patterns that influence our feelings and behaviors, uncovering psychological strategies or defense mechanisms that our unconscious minds use to protect our self and socially acceptable image and help us cope.

34 See chapter III.

35 See chapter III.

36 Parallel world is a concept that comes from quantum physics. Parallel worlds means that a diversity of worlds exists simultaneously.

By examining the source of the patterns, psychotherapy can reduce the anxiety and allow for more choice. Process oriented therapies observe the simultaneous existence of parallel conscious realities that move us forward. They explore the various manifestations of the unconscious and conscious and bring them into a dialogue, dance and relationship.

To frame our understanding of Process, Arnold Mindell, a pioneering process thinker and therapist, developed an experiential map with three levels: consensus reality, dreaming and essence (see Table 1). Consensus reality is the culturally sanctioned level of reality with it's agreed upon norms and values. Consensus reality is the world of objects and parts. It also demarcates the experiences that are deemed to be outside of the realm of social norms that are considered abnormal or pathological, and thus are marginalized by most people or treated to regain a place of conformity. Dreaming consists of experiences that elude our willful intent or agency. All the dreaming experiences (body symptoms, night dreams, relationship conflicts, altered states and world interactions) are subjective. They escape the control of our brain CEO; they alter our conscious intentions and primary sense of self or primary identity. They are parallel-world experiences and as such they expose marginalized aspects of our process and are a source of developmental wisdom. They are the stranger within and without ourselves that scares us and challenges us to expand our range of consciousness and identity. They disturb our comfort zone and call us to engage with our diversity. At the essence or transpersonal level, experiences are subtle, fleeting and difficult to verbalize. Experiences here are the acorn from which the whole oak tree arises. They are the roots and kernels of our consensus reality and dreaming experiences. Mindell speaks about experiences in this realm as being beyond ordinary space and time and "non-local." They transcend the realm of conventional physics and matter and connect us to what some call God, nature, spirit, soul and processmind.

Using a parallel-world framework infers that these levels of experience are interconnected and that we can move from one to the other. All levels are relevant and need to be examined for their value in any specific situation or context. If you have an accident and fracture a limb, you need the consensus reality skills of a good surgeon to redress the bones and stabilize them with a cast or external pins. After that, exploring the dreaming and essence level experiences might help put the accident into a larger meaning context.

### Table 1: Three Levels of Experience

> Consensus Reality/Primary Identity: Culturally sanctioned aspects of reality and the way we integrate them in our identity. They include who we are, what we do and how we identify ourselves. They also incorporate conventional medical views about health and normality, allopathic and naturopathic medical practices, diagnosis, treatments, etc. An individual will speak about the practical or factual aspects of her life and when talking about her community she will mention the issues and problems they face.
>
> Dreaming/Secondary Identity: Our term for the field of subjective experiences, including unintentional processes in our bodies, dreams and images that accompany us throughout our lives, emotions and reactions we have to people and the atmospheres we sense around them. These experiences give us indications about our secondary processes. In a team, group or community individuals will mention people in certain roles and how they feel affected by them, the atmosphere they experience and the conflicts that are present.
>
> Essence/Transpersonal: The realm of non-dualistic transpersonal experiences. Observer and observed, sick and healthy, doctor and patient are one unit. As an observer, it refers to a state in which you feel your way into the person's experience. It reflects an experience in which you have the sense of joining the person in his or her world, rather than feeling like an outsider. As an individual we feel a sense of being grounded and at home and that we share a common humanity with our peers.

An old Greek myth recounts how travelers on the road to Athens, the cultural and political center of ancient Greece, regularly stopped at an inn. The innkeeper, Procrustes, said to be the son of Poseidon, was an ogre and offered only one size of bed to rest on. At night when the travelers were asleep, Procrustes would come into their rooms and cut off any part of them that would not fit on the bed. If they were too short for the bed, he would stretch them until they fit.

This myth is a metaphor for what happens to us as we, all throughout life, adjust to the one size bed of mainstream consensus reality. We stretch and cut off parts of ourselves to fit cultural values and norms. To function as a community, we use Procrustes to agree on what reality is; he helps us abide by certain conventions and, for example, drive on the same side of the road. Without conventions and norms, chaos and suffering would ensue. Yet, the pressure of normality and conventions, our internalized procrustean bed, creates pathology. It creates tension for those who are different and don't fit certain cultural norms and expectations.

This consensus reality is an important reality, but it is not the only one. Albert Einstein said: "Reality is merely an illusion, although a very persistent one." His relativity theory postulates that reality is only relative and has a brief lifetime. Both the mass and the length of an object depend on its speed relative to another object. Since objects in the real world are always moving at slightly different speeds relative to one another and from one instant of time to the next, reality constantly changes. If we contemplate the illusionary aspect of our agreed-upon reality and instead use a parallel-world or multiple-reality framework, we open ourselves to our inner diversity and the diversity of the world and the communities around us.

Mindell suggests that, for the most part, we marginalize the dreaming and essence levels of reality and orient all our experiences to consensus reality: "We look only for the most probable meaning of something ... Metaphorically speaking, looking only at the real value of an experience gives us answers in reality, but ignores the sentient dreamlike experiences and process of reflection behind reality... Consensus reality is like a tree with roots in the non-consensus or sentient realm" (2000, 111).

If we go back to the myth of Procrustes and include what Mindell suggests, this is how we all function on a daily basis: we live life with one reality in mind, apply ourselves to getting ahead and cope with all the demands and expectations that we perceive are asked from us. We start to push and neglect our own needs. Initially conflicts arise in relationship, at work or within our families. Then we become sick or have an accident; somehow our bodies get involved. Later, if we continue on the same path, we develop problems in the world—we might lose our jobs or develop a serious illness. This can be a wake-up call and the beginning of our healing process. We start to reorganize our lives, reinvent ourselves and reconnect with our life goals and purpose.

We all go through the cycle described above many times, at least through the initial steps. To marginalize aspects of our lives that are creative and spiritual is normal; we all do it. Our lives are amply filled with everyday tasks of making a living, raising children, staying healthy, being partners and lovers, etc. We relegate our creative and spiritual needs to Sunday mornings or other specific worship times, weekends and vacations. A cold or flu is then a natural reaction and compensation for a lifestyle that has little or no down time. With increasing levels of stress, when our everyday tasks are burdened by poverty, isolation, family tensions, racial and other social conflicts, it gets harder to stay healthy and more serious or chronic health problems surface. Many of these causes are social in nature and require community-wide advocacy to reduce environmental stressors. In these situations, we can't address health issues only from an individual perspective; this is not sufficient.

Individually, illness and disease provoke fear and uncertainty. They throw us off balance and out of our ordinary lives. We are forced to confront our boundaries, limitations and vulnerabilities. If we have the privilege we can use the experience of illness and follow its course, let the altered state guide us out of the ordinary into the dreaming and sentient world. To give ourselves that space is a luxury, and many times we will choose to take a pill and go back to our everyday lives.

For better understanding Process and the life cycles described above we must explore signal and field theory.

## *Signal Theory (Semiotics)*

A sign or signal is everything that carries communication and meaning between two objects or parties. Sign processes and signal-based communication occur on verbal and non-verbal levels. DNA sequences, for example, constitute signs and codes that help the cell in producing amino acids and proteins. Cellular antigens and antibodies mediate the body's immune response. Neurotransmitters bridge the communication between two nerve cells. Physiologic body reactions transmit affective information. Body symptoms are signs of underlying physical processes and motivate us to rest, take some medicine or consult a medical professional. Verbal cues and language then expand the communication on the cognitive levels and allow for the interpretation of subjective experiences, symbols, metaphors and stories. Signs are ubiquitous and flood us with conscious and subconscious information. They can come as paired verbal and non-verbal cues which can be coherent or contradictory. An inconsistent pair of signs is called a double-signal. They carry different meanings and can be very confusing. In general we assign verbal information more validity and tend to overlook the other conflicting signals. It then becomes the source of miscommunication and conflict. Sign processes are also the foundation of fields and field forces which we will examine next.

## *Field Theory*

Fields are spheres of influence, geographical areas, a region in space with certain characteristics such as magnetism, a set of mathematical elements that follow certain rules, a complex of forces that influence human behavior, etc. Fields have applications in physics, mathematics and social psychology. They determine certain conditions and rules and pattern behavior. The Gestalt[37] psychologist Kurt Lewin coined the term "group dynamics" and defined behavior (B) as a function of the person (P) in their environment (E): $B = f(P, E)$. He described groups as having supervening qualities that cannot be understood from an individual perspective alone. In consensus reality (CR), we are separate individuals with personal histories and individual psychologies. In a group we adopt certain roles based on certain characteristics such as birth order, gender, class, education and rank. Conventional role theory says that we behave out of these socially defined roles such as parent, lover, manager, teacher, etc. Our roles come with a set of socially defined rights, norms, expectations and behaviors. Lewin added that groups and roles are shaped by field forces. These forces constellate the dynamics in a group independent from the individual. We all experience that field force when we enter a certain group or system, it can

37 Gestalt psychology (Gestalt is German for "essence or shape of an entity's complete form") is a theory of mind and brain that sees the brain as holistic with self-organizing tendencies. Gestalt therapists focus on patterns and the whole before examining individual parts, suggesting the whole is greater than the sum of its parts.

pull us to step into a certain role or take certain viewpoints. The group has a force field that co-determines our behavior. If you go back into the system of your family of origin you will experience that suddenly you may behave as if time has stopped and you returned to your childhood.

Arnold Mindell (2000) went further and described how these roles and forces are unaffected by individuals and are interchangeable. If one individual steps out of a role, the group's force field will look for another individual to take on that role. This group governing force field has non consensus reality (NCR) qualities.

Consensual aspects of groups based on role and rank theory are not enough to explain group dynamics. Moods, attitudes and beliefs tangle us together; they are shared and, like a magnet, they organize us. Even roles that are not present in the room virtually contribute to the force field and determine the group's behavior. These virtual or ghost roles come up through gossip, through being mentioned as third parties and through a person's dreams. The group's or communities' force fields pattern our behaviors to bring awareness to its vision, goal or direction.

Imagine an organization. The birth of the organization results from an idea, purpose or vision. That idea is often made explicit in the organization's mission statement. A school has the mission to educate, a hospital to foster healing, a business to deliver some services and goods and to make some profit, etc. The organization's mission or vision exerts a powerful organizing force; it brings people together, creates jobs and provides medicine and education. That system's or organization's force is bigger than any one individual or member of the group. It will survive beyond the existence of the organization. That force field is like the music that an orchestra plays. Sometimes it can be dissonant, loud or muted. But it will remain the same music independent from the specific orchestra or musician. Some musicians and orchestras are better players; nevertheless, the essence of the music remains the same.

Psychological field theories have huge implications for medicine. The medical field forces create the music of the patient–provider relationship, as well as the relationship between the hospital, group practice, agency administration and provider, families, care teams, etc.

As providers and patients we learn to play our individual instruments and become experts in our roles. We rarely have the opportunity to learn to play and tune into the bigger music. Later, I will describe ways one can develop some awareness about the music and force field that organizes our behavior as a patient or provider. But first, let us explore special aspects of the music, which are beliefs and attitudes.

## *The Role of Beliefs*

From a process oriented perspective, beliefs are an intrinsic part of our experience and they have a strong influence on how we treat our bodies, how we think about health and how we relate to structures and systems that help us on our recovery journey. Beliefs are powerful and infectious. They are the building blocks of our cultures. They shape our thoughts and actions, our relationships and community efforts. They are non-local in the sense of being shared by individuals, communities and whole cultures. They form the philosophies and paradigms that inform our thinking and attitudes about life, social interactions and lifestyle choices. They create the field we live in and guide the roles that represent the polarities of the field. In an ongoing subliminal process of consensus building, they shape what we experience as reality, true or false, right or wrong. They are externally represented through the media and religious and scientific institutions, and we also experience them through internalized representations of our parents, teachers and peers. They are good and bad medicine, placebo and nocebo[38]. In health, they shape our hopes and despairs and organize our physiologies.

In the 1970s, breast cancer was believed to be deadly, and many women died shortly after their initial diagnosis. Breast cancer is now much more treatable, and the change in attitude toward breast cancer has added to the reduction of its mortality. New treatments bestow hope and change our beliefs and survival rates.

In his book *Man's Search for Meaning*, Viktor Frankl (2006), a Jewish psychiatrist and Holocaust survivor of the Nazi prison camps of Theresienstadt, Auschwitz and Tuerkheim, found that if you have a goal then your chances of survival improves. He came to the crucial conclusion that if you can find some meaning even in the most painful, absurd and dehumanizing situation, then you can develop inner powers and resources that give you a better chance of overcoming the challenges you face. To maintain his own feelings of meaning and purpose, Frankl

38 See also chapter VI.

imagined delivering lectures to his students and in his mind wrote the books he later published. He found that life is teleological; it is goal-oriented and directed toward a final result.

The United States lost more prisoners of war in the Korean War than in any other war. The casualty rate was about 40 percent. The North Korean and Chinese Communists used elaborate methods of indoctrination, which took away hope from the captives. Both in Nazi prison camps and in Korean or Chinese internment camps, prisoners who lost hope frequently crawled into a corner or into their bunk beds, pulled a blanket over their heads and died within 48 hours—some overnight from no apparent physical cause. In many cultures, individuals may be punished by a collective process of social expulsion or ostracism, a fate often practically equivalent to death. These examples demonstrate that hope and the belief in a meaningful existence is a central life force. When they are taken away, it can be deadly.

For about 10 years now, I have been working with a middle-aged woman who has been rejected and ostracized by her family. As the oldest she protected her mother and siblings from an abusive alcoholic father from a very early age onwards. She would stand in front of him to give her mother time to collect the younger ones and run away. She endured innumerable beatings and later on extreme sexual abuse. She continues to be the scapegoat of her family of origin, as well as her own two sons. She has internalized most of the blame and engages in multiple self-destructive behaviors. She is chronically depressed and suicidal and suffers from debilitating physical health issues. She has almost no hope, and it's a wonder she has survived so far.

Antonovsky (1979) studied hope in a different context. He studied women who had survived both the Holocaust and the subsequent displacement and immigration to Israel, major life stressors that would normally result in impaired health. In his research, he discovered a subgroup of women who seemed to have extraordinary resilience in facing these major life challenges. A characteristic of these women was that they were able to maintain a sense that their life path was somehow predictable and explicable, that they had the resources to manage the challenges and that the life demands were worthy of investment and engagement. He termed this psychological and spiritual power *sense of coherence*. According to Antonovsky, if a person believes there is no reason to persist and survive and confront challenges, and if she has no sense of meaning and direction, then she will lose the motivation to strive and live. In his research he demonstrated that, in contrast, a strong sense of coherence predicts positive health outcomes.

To summarize: if you have no supportive relationships, if you have no hope, goal or sense of direction and meaning, you get sick and die. In contrast, love, hope and meaning are excellent medicine. My work with the client mentioned above consists of mainly trying to instill hope against all odds. Over the years, what has worked best is to help her connect with some place on earth that she can call home. She often returns in her mind to a special Oregon beach where she feels at home and connected to a deeper ground.

Signs, fields and beliefs inform Process, the stream of constantly changing relationships between parts, states and patterns. They also constitute the foundation for the process oriented methods that I want to describe next. I think they can be useful in tackling the individual and community dimensions of health.

## *Process oriented Methods*

Process oriented approaches have evolved into a diversified methodology and psychotherapeutic practice with applications in medicine, psychiatry, individual counseling, couples counseling, organizational and community development, conflict facilitation and mediation. Their philosophies are fundamentally positive, as they believe in a meaningful process that manifests itself continuously in manifold "dreamlike" ways such as illness, complexes, relationship difficulties and social conflicts. They are painful and in need of healing or alleviation. They are also an opportunity for bringing awareness into the parallel world and dreaming reality and a potential for enriching growth and development.

Process oriented methods and attitudes believe in inner and outer diversity as a path toward compassionate understanding of oneself and the world. They are deeply evolutionary in their quest for meaning and community building.

One source of process oriented thinking in psychotherapy stems from Arnold Mindell, who I have mentioned previously. His endless curiosity and interest allowed him to integrate physics, social sciences and psychology. As I shared in chapter II, Jung's collaborator Marie

Louise von Franz encouraged him to study the relationship between dreams and body symptoms, and this became the initial step of an ongoing journey into the world of night dreams and living dreams, the manifestation of dreaming in relationship difficulties, physical symptoms, altered states, coma and world conflicts.

Mindell's path led him to study psychology, become a training analyst at the Jung institute in Zurich, found his own school of psychology (process oriented psychology or Processwork), develop methods of working with large groups and organizations (worldwork and deep democracy) and finally to return to physics and apply quantum mechanics to medicine and the body. He is now considered the most innovative Jungian theorist and the most read Jungian author, and in 2012 the United States Association for Body Psychotherapy recognized him as a pioneer of Body Psychotherapy.

Following are some process oriented concepts and methods that are germane to the discussion and exploration of health and sickness.

### Dreambody

The dreambody is a concept Mindell developed in the early 1970s. In his words:

> The dreambody appears as sentient, generally unrecognized sensations that eventually manifest in dream images, body experiences, and symptoms. The dreaming bridges the gap between our measurable, physical bodies and the immeasurable experience of the so-called mind. What we see in our dreams we feel in our bodies. Likewise, what we experience in our bodies we can find in our dreams (1984, 64).

Dreams and body experiences come together: every nighttime dream is connected to a body experience, and every body experience can be visualized and usually appears in a dream. If a symptom feels like a pressure, it is likely that people or characters that pressure you will appear in the person's dreams. Similarly, we dream of one state and wake up in a mood and with some physical experience. Dreambody means that all the various parallel states, worlds or bodies are present in a given moment. But in waking life, we have a tendency to marginalize many of the more subtle states and concentrate on our everyday personality and identity.

Later, Mindell expanded his dreambody concept by incorporating quantum physics into his research about body symptoms and medicine. He was interested in the question: how does a symptom such as pressure feel *before* it becomes a medically relevant symptom? He found out that the subtle feeling experiences at the core of a symptom relate to the deeper psychological and spiritual aspects of a person's identity and process. At the essence or processmind level, the spiritual and material come together. He differentiates between the everyday world of practical activities, in which consensual views of reality reign, and a more symbolic numinous realm that is governed by dreamlike events. Symptoms are seen as an attempt to compensate for the one-sidedness of consensual reality and as a link to the world of sentient experiences. Mainstream views structure our experience of normality, what we perceive as functional or dysfunctional, normal or deviant, healthy or unhealthy. Normality influences the way we feel about certain groups of people (e.g., the elderly) and various types of bodies (e.g., thin or obese, ill or diseased). These doctrines that arise from social dialogue are subjected to power struggles within competing social groups and interests with some dominating over others and defining what counts as "truth."

From Mindell's standpoint, the most marginalized aspect of today's discourse about life and experience of life is the realm of dreaming. Materialistic views dominate our current perception and experience of reality. From quantum physics, he extrapolates a dimension of experience in which time is non-linear and parts, events and ideas are entangled and non-local. In this sentient dimension, basic tendencies, moods and atmospheric changes reign. Subtle influences and energies resonate throughout our bodies and manifest in slight discomforts and symptoms at the fringe of our awareness. They can later develop into full-blown symptoms and diseases. Quantum or sentient medicine's aim, says Mindell (2000), is to discover the origin of problems before they manifest as symptoms.

We focus on the dominant CR tone and marginalize the NCR sub- and over-tones. But our essence is the sum of all our sub-tones and states. We feel best if we don't marginalize our over-tones. When all facets of our body experiences are combined, we feel like we are on the right path. Dreambody refers to the mystery that's beyond the physical realm and includes the physical body we experience moment by moment.

One way of experiencing the mystery is to ask the question: What is this body that I am experiencing? We can describe it as something we see, as an experience of a feeling or a movement or analyze it as comprising various chemical components. We can subjectively feel a body symptom as: "a drilling inside my head," "a red-hot poker feeling that is constant both in my head and jaw," "a pressure that wants to come out of my body," "a pressure on my chest that stops me from breathing," etc.

But, can we ever say what it *is*? At this level, we can refer to the dreambody as: the Tao, the Self (Jung), the Mysterium Tremendum (Rudolph Otto), God, Consciousness, Ground of Being or the sentient realm. It manifests as the vital energy ("élan vital"—Bergson 1911), connecting the entirety of the universe. Bohm uses the term implicate order and Rupert Sheldrake describes it as the morphogenetic field, the underlying pattern manifesting in particular bodily forms.

From a general perspective, the dreambody, is the process of dreaming or the organizing principle in the background. The specific dreambody shows up in people's experiences in three parallel bodies:

1. The CR (consensus reality) body is the physical body, with its material, biological and physiological processes—the body of our skin, fluids, organs and bones. The body we take care of through our diet, taking our supplements, exercising, going to the doctors or other health care practitioners, etc.

2. The vital or dreaming body refers to the subjective and energetic quality of our physical experience. This might include the burning and itching sensations accompanying a rash or nighttime dreams of a fiery and scratching cat, for example.

3. The essence body is the experience of a guiding force or general direction in life. It expresses itself in flirts and tendencies, a felt sense we can't quite describe in words.

While we distinguish between the physical, vital or dreaming and essence bodies, we cannot make any absolute separation between them. We can describe them as co-inhering or overlapping in one another. At the same time, as we experience ourselves in parallel worlds or in super-positions of these parallel worlds, some practices allow us to distinguish between them. They help us examine the meaning of our individual symptom or body Process.

## Disturber (X) and Disturbed (Y)

One simple way to examine the dreaming process is to explore the subjective experience of the body symptom (call it the "sick" you, or X energy) and the experience of the part in you that gets disturbed by it (call it the "healthy" you, or Y energy). First, amplify the subjective experience of the symptom and synthesize it into a hand or arm gesture (i.e., the pounding of a fist expressing a headache) and/or a brief sketch on a piece of paper that captures the energetic quality of the experience. Then, ask yourself what part in you is bothered, disturbed or troubled by that qualitative expression of the symptom energy. This is the part of you that would rather go on with life as is and not be deranged, the part that wants to stay calm, balanced, etc. Then, unfold and express that second experience in a gesture or sketch and compare both experiences. Let them dialogue with each other, and explore if you can find a way to dance between or with both experiences, embracing them as aspects of who you are in the moment.

Try drawing both sketches on a medicine or pill container. They will represent what you are trying to regain and what you are fighting. It will allow you to have a better understanding of the overall process, the parallel worlds of your consensus reality and dreaming identity. You can do this little exercise with every symptom or medication you take. The sketches represent the state you want to achieve by taking the pill and the state you are fighting.

## Finding Your Home

One of our biggest problems is that we think we ought to be this or that. In so doing, we marginalize other aspects of ourselves, and symptoms become something we don't agree with. We can address the consensus reality difficulties that symptoms have and use medicine, exercise, massage, herbal supplements, etc., while examining the dreaming qualities. We can also focus on finding the common or essence ground, our own sense of feeling at ease, at home and being enough, by remembering a special place on earth in which we feel at home and well. Imagine returning to that place in your mind and look around. Explore that place and how it creates in you a sense of home. Discern the various elements that shape that place and imagine embodying them individually and as a whole. Become that place and shift your gaze toward yourself and let the earth speak to you through that experience of wholeness and wellness. Often, when you look at yourself on that special place on earth that feels so much like home, and you look around, that place will depict qualities that are also yours (i.e., the ocean a soothing quality, the rocks a more steadfast quality etc.).You will find the various superpositional experiences of your X and Y energies in some of the elements that organize your home spot on earth.

## Playing the Music

As providers, when we are disconnected from the music, we have a tendency to burn out. As patients, we might become hopeless and depressed. There is nothing wrong with being depressed and burned out. These feelings will actually help you reconnect with the music, your personal unbroken wholeness, processmind or common ground. On the other hand, it might also benefit you to prevent this experience. As a provider, organization or group your behavior is motivated by a calling or vision. You might revisit your mission statement for inspiration or you might want to write one for yourself if you haven't yet done so. What is your specific vision and why is it calling you?

To address your burn out or depression, first identify what disturbs you: what creates the burned out feeling or sense of hopelessness? Is it a specific person, patient, doctor, family member, boss, supervisor, administrator, employee, a specific role or expectation, a certain loss, a sense of feeling victimized, etc? Examine that imagined person, role, belief or expectation and express its disturbing characteristic in a motion, gesture, sound or sketch/drawing. Let yourself be creative in expressing that experience. Next, do the same for the part in you that gets disturbed by that first experience. If you feel burned out or depressed, let yourself be pulled down[39]; don't fight the experience but let it guide you where it wants to go, and again, express it creatively. Then examine your personal or organizational mission statement as a professional, team, family or individual. Can you express the essence of your mission statement? Lastly, bring all these various experiences into a dance, tune, poem or drawing and let them speak to you and give you

39 If you suffer from clinical depression, please do this with the help of your counselor.

a new direction. In what ways do they work together? In what ways do they conflict? What are they saying to you?

### Abuse Work

Another aspect of working on health-related issues has to do with our behaviors, feelings, projections and beliefs and those of our environment. We feel marginalized, misunderstood or oppressed by family members, members of our care teams or the community as a whole. We internalize their expectations and values as inner critics and self-demeaning, self-defeating thoughts and behaviors, and we know how they influence our sense of well-being and health. To return to an inner place of "I am good enough, as is, independent of ifs, shoulds and whens," it can be helpful to examine an underlying abuse issue. Choose one simple experience in which you felt somehow oppressed or abused by another person or situation. Remember how you felt and what or who created that feeling in you. Then imagine how you would react today in that situation with all your abilities and faculties that you now have. With a friend or helper, play act that past abuse situation and your response to it from the person you are today.

### Addictions

Cravings and addictions are powerful processes that devastate our bodies and are very hard to overcome. They make us feel ashamed and guilty and are linked with depression and anxiety. They are connected with inner and outer beliefs and judgments. In a process oriented paradigm, they are seen as altered states or dreaming experiences that balance unfulfilled, one-sided lifestyles. A workaholic with high expectations might crave relaxation and be pulled into using a drug or substance to help relax. Someone with subtle depression might crave the dopamine high and sense of well-being that one can achieve through over-eating or over-exercising. Someone else with a sense of loneliness and lack of deep-feeling connections can crave sex in an attempt to find a loving connection. We project compensating states and powers onto substances and behaviors. To reclaim the power of the projection, imagine the essence of the specific craving or addiction: the sense of letting go that exhaling smoke can provide, the sweetness in a cookie, the detachment and dreaming in alcohol and other drugs. Use your creativity to examine the experience the substance or behavior gives you and integrate that power in your everyday life.

## Rank and Diversity

Individual privileges and social rankings affect our sense of wellness, empowerment and ability to face health challenges. The lacks of these also cause disease and illness. Our bodies and emotional states are the symbolic battlefield of political forces that discriminate over others and influence access to resources and care. Rank differences exist between patients and providers. A process oriented paradigm includes examining these dynamics as part of the individual work on disease and body symptoms. Health education comprises giving individuals access to information and knowledge and supporting them to improve their social standing and powers. It involves supporting individual beliefs and health practices, as well as coaching individuals how to communicate with providers and advocate for a holistic response and care.

Knowing that good intentions are not enough, mainstream health education consists of behavioral strategies to overcome our brain's tendencies to be seduced by short-term gains over long-term goals; this is especially useful for dealing with cravings and addictions[40]. These strategies emphasize minimizing temptations, establishing contracts that bind our future behaviors (i.e., the Ulysses contract[41]), recruiting social pressure, putting money on the line and involving emotions. A process oriented paradigm adopts these consensus reality behavioral strategies and adds examining the deeper meanings of health-related processes to health coaching and education. Besides doing so on an individual level, I also suggest using community forums to address the social and cultural dimensions of health education and coaching. Two additional community dialogue methods are part of the process oriented practices. They are used in settings with larger groups and are well suited for addressing the social and cultural aspects of health and sickness.

## Group Process

From a process oriented perspective, organizations and communities are living organisms with feelings, beliefs, visions and dreams. Group

40 See chapter III for the neuroscientific explanation of this.

41 Ulysses ordered his men to securely lash him to the mast of his ship to prevent him from succumbing to the devastating lure of the beautiful Sirens' song. We make behavioral contracts to counter the detrimental actions of our future selves we assume will succumb to cravings and other impulses.

process is the method used to explore not only the rational facts of community problems that require practical solutions but also the relational feelings, the creative diversity, the aspirations and hopes and the irrational non-local forces that guide us as individuals and groups. Group process brings to the forefront the marginalized roles that shape our communication and feelings. Group Process uses deep democracy[42] principles to examine the roles that are present in a group and help facilitate dialogue and resolutions. Roles are seen as shared by everyone and a manifestation of the dreaming of the group, team or community. They are governed and structured by field forces. Like a magnetic field, the background field of a group or team creates polarized roles to bring awareness to the group's and team's processes. The diversity expressed in polarized roles allows for conflict and learning. As individuals, we have tendencies to fill and represent certain roles—but the roles themselves are bigger than any one individual, and as individuals we are much more than one specific role. The sick and disabled, for example, bring some times awareness to the group about vulnerability, life's uncertainty and our common humanness. Their sickness is only one part of their overall process and the sick role is only one aspect of their overall identity.

No one inhabits just one role and all of us can step or be pulled into a specific role depending on the context and the atmosphere of a group. Based on this role theory, a crucial aspect of group work is discovering the various aspects of a group that manifest through roles. Some roles are more welcomed than others, and certain roles will go underground and become ghost-like. Group members will gossip about these roles but will be very reluctant to stand openly for them. In group process, representing these ghost roles can be very helpful in facilitating the group's overt and hidden agenda, direction and vision.

## Open Forum

Open forums are based on the premise that community participation helps flatten hierarchies and strengthen democratic processes. They are public events that host discussions about community issues. They are ideal settings for a community to get to know the diversity of ideas and feelings of its members. Every culture and community has its own tradition of public events, where the voices of the community are invited

42 See chapter V.

to express themselves. These include town hall meetings, gatherings for storytelling and sharing food and those held by faith-based congregations to bare common values and beliefs.

A process oriented paradigm uses open forums as a method for processing community issues and conflicts. Individuals from opposing and polarized roles are identified and invited to share their view of a certain topic. In a recent public forum on climate change I attended in Portland, scientists presented their views on the urgency of the issue and the need for green measures to avert catastrophic changes in our environment. Representatives from a political think tank, which questions the validity of the scientific perspective, shared their views. At times a deep conflictual dialogue ensued. People listened to each other and found their common responsibility for taking care of the environment. The group came together and discussed the science, psychology, art and spirituality of the environment and community making. The forum allowed those involved to address the problem of climate change and became an opportunity to discover shared responsibilities and the need for community building.

In an open forum on health equity I organized in Portland in 2010, 65 participants from various backgrounds gathered. There were providers and individuals identified as "patients," or people who suffered from health disparities. One participant spoke from a perspective of a cancer survivor and mother of a mentally ill son. She spoke about the need to advocate for one's own health needs and blamed doctors for not always being responsive enough. Another participant spoke from the perspective of having been a nurse practitioner and now an assistant professor at a local nursing school. She emphasized the need to connect with one's humanness. A staff member from a local county commissioner's office spoke about health being much more than an individual problem and she emphasized the need to address the social issues that contribute to poor health. The open discussion that followed circled around various topics, such as the need for community building, connecting at a human level and overcoming a sense of isolation and marginalization. Some participants blamed health care providers, social structures and policies and the insurance and pharmaceutical companies for delivering poor services and fostering social injustice which contributes to poor health. Some expressed frustration and hopelessness and a sense of feeling that they had no voice. Some compared the

American health care system to other health care systems, complaining about the American one being ineffective and too costly. In answer to the complaints and blame, some young nursing students expressed pride in their profession and the successes that they see possible in the United States. The health disparities were contrasted with the richness of the diverse voices there, which included those filled with humor, sadness and anger.

Further discussion ensued about how to be healthy as individuals and communities, how to take care of ourselves and our communities, how to empower underserved communities by using a Community Health Worker (CHW) model and how to advocate and find answers to the multiple problems. Participants stressed the need for more prevention, as well as the necessity for policy change to ensure equal access to affordable care and insurance coverage. At the end, two participants from socially marginalized subgroups expressed the fact that everybody needs a hand, even a doctor, even the president.

In that forum, many roles were expressed, such as the one who is a victim, a sufferer, in pain, hopeless and powerless. Other roles were the doctor, who at times abuses his or her rank and is unaware of his or her privileges but is also a helper. More hidden or ghost roles were the insurance companies and the pharmaceutical companies who make profit or the self-centered individualist who is egotistical and doesn't care about others. In contrast to the victim, the empowered individual came forward, as well as the proud nurse or health care provider. Underneath there was also a reflection on community, that "everybody needs a hand" and that we all share a common humanness. Lastly, some participants expressed the views of detached elders who have lived through all with humor, sadness and anger.

Group process and open forums are places for conflict and dialogue. They bear witness to the diversity of groups, teams and communities and foster the exchange of thoughts, feelings and actions. They are venues to explore the groups' issues, parts and divisiveness and to address and implement solutions. They also uncover the groups' dreaming and deeper vision. They often reveal the groups' process and help build community and mutual understanding. In individual work, we examine parts and identities, as well as patterns and overall life paths. In group work, the parts express themselves as roles. By processing the roles we can reach a common ground of mutual respect, learning and trust building. Collective action, policy advocacy and change can result but are not the main focus.

## CONCLUSION

A process oriented medicine sees illness and disease as the breakdown of our complex adaptive system we call health. Together our psychologies, brains and immune systems work together in a constant exchange of information with the environment to create a state of balance or good-enough health. Multiple layers of feedback systems allow us to adjust our physiologies to the constant changes we are encountering on a minute-to-minute and day-to-day basis. This ability to maintain a stable internal environment through physiologic, behavioral and social changes has been named allostasis[43] and is one major characteristic of good health.

Faced with too much stress, challenge and change our systems break down and we get sick. As in other complex systems this process follows non-linear rules, which means that small causes can have a big effect once our health-protecting systems become sufficiently unstable. Nobody can predict exactly when we will get sick or who will get sick when facing a certain threat such as, a virus or some toxin that alters our DNA and creates cancer. Imagine adding sand to a sandpile in the shape of a cone. Over time, the sides of the pyramid get steeper and at some point a sand slide becomes inevitable—but nobody can predict when adding just a single grain of sand will trigger an avalanche.

Our complex state of health is deeply unpredictable. Health is a poised critical state that minor disturbances can tip out of balance and create disease states of all sizes, like avalanches of sand in a sandpile. We live constantly on the edge of unpredictable change. Health is a dynamic interactive process and requires ongoing complex adjusting behaviors.

Restoring health, once we get sick, requires certain medical procedures or treatments, some lifestyle changes such as dietary or exercise regimens and the strengthening of our allostasis or ability to adapt to the changes and uncertainty of life. Resilience is our positive capacity

43 Allostasis means remaining stable through change. It is the body's internal process of achieving stability, or homeostasis, while undergoing physiological or behavioral change.

to adjust to change and cope with life challenges and stress. This adjustment and learning process may result in our "bouncing back" to health or using the adverse experience to become stronger and more resilient (much like a vaccine gives us the capacity to cope well with future exposure to disease). Resilience is a very individual process that depends on individual and cultural values and belief systems. In addition, resilience can be strengthened through finding and creating meaning and coherence by examining the symptoms' dreaming process and how it relates to our overall force field or processmind.

In process oriented medicine, individualized recovery goals may include:

- □ Cultivating inspiration for our creativity.
- □ Encouraging us to see change as healing and believe that healing is change.
- □ Reminding us that our humor and curiosity will help us through illness.
- □ Helping us find purpose and direction.
- □ Strengthening our sense of feeling at home even when in pain and suffering.
- □ Developing a space for learning and community.
- □ Inspiring us to think on our own and believe in our experiences and ourselves.
- □ Fostering our confidence in caring for ourselves.
- □ Nurturing our belief in our self-healing powers and the flow of nature they bring to life.
- □ Instilling our trust in our true and deepest nature.
- □ Shaping a better world for us, our family and our community.
- □ Supporting our internal diversity and the diversity of our communities.
- □ Exploring our own powers of creative healing.

The need for accountability and effectiveness shape current medical practices. They include the requirement to base these practices on scientific evidence and the pressure to produce positive outcomes. Social dynamics that exclude some from significant economic and educational resources and cultural ideas about beauty, age and the body are iatrogenic[44]. These dynamics and ideas are co-creators of disease and illness. A process oriented healing paradigm addresses the physical challenges and various iatrogenic systems, as well as fostering resilience and meaning in examining the dreambody and connecting it to the individual force field. Experts and patients are roles in a larger field, shared by everybody, embodied by one person or another at any specific point in time. What is normal is subjective, a group process constantly shifting. Normal is useful as it guides our awareness about our health and helps identify treatments to help us stay healthy. And it is only one viewpoint under many multiple simultaneous truths.

A process oriented understanding of medicine sees:

- □ Life is a process unfolding toward learning, awareness and growth (teleology/dreaming). This process includes aspects of both consensus reality (CR) and non-consensus reality (NCR).
- □ The "bug" (disease, conflict, disturbance) is the initial spark for consciousness. It contains the solution.
- □ Experience is multi-modal; it includes aspects of consensus reality, dreaming and sentient levels.
- □ With increased awareness you have more choice and can be more fluid.
- □ Diversity (inner and outer) is an essential aspect of life. It is necessary for more awareness and mutual learning. Rank is an essential aspect of experience.
- □ Parallel worlds, non-locality and complementarity mean that everything is shared; the boundaries are fluid and fuzzy. Interpersonal relationships are part of the whole.
- □ Medicine is both individual and public/collective. Group process and open forums are integral parts of medicine.

---

44 An iatrogenic event is an inadvertent adverse effect or complication resulting from medical treatment or advice. I am using the term here in a larger cultural context to describe the side effects of social and cultural dynamics.

- Interventions are guided by Process awareness and feedback.

Health and sickness are processes with many facets. They include individual and collective factors. To understand the individual experience of health it is important to be knowledgeable and aware of health's embedding in sociocultural systems. This is what I will explore in the next chapter.

5

# *Deep Democracy and Health*

*Of all of the forms of inequality, injustice in health is the most shocking and the most inhumane.*

Martin Luther King, Jr.

Let's turn our attention to the social and cultural embedding of health. Health and sickness are subjective experiences that take place in a social and cultural context. They are both private and public. As deeply subjective experiences, they escape social control and regulation. Social institutions, on the other hand, invest huge amounts of resources into the safeguard of the health and well-being of its members and are responsible for their just distribution. The subjectivity of health and sickness opens the door to the abuse of social assistance and entitlement benefits. Whereas if society excludes all ill people from social security benefits in whom one finds no objectifiable signs of a disease, there is a risk of injustice. Lack of recognition and understanding about specific disease processes and kinds of suffering keep some people away from having access to their justified resources and benefits.

Our embedding in a social nervous system and the intertwining of the sociobiological system forces us to think about health and sickness as a collective issue and not only a private one. We affect each other and are changed by society. Social dynamics of power, rank and diversity directly affect people's health and their chance to stay well. Hence, a comprehensive discussion of health and sickness has to address the public and collective dimensions of health. At the end of the last chapter, I explored some community-based practices that facilitate dialogue and community participation. In this chapter, I examine some additional concepts and ideas that speak to the social and cultural elements of health and sickness.

## *Deep Democracy*

In this section I will concentrate on rank, diversity, healthism and health disparities, but I want to start with the theoretical construct of deep democracy. Deep democracy is a political philosophy, a way of working with people and groups and a particular feeling and attitude toward the diversity of individual and group dynamics. Arnold Mindell first described this concept in his book *The Leader as a Martial Artist* (2000). Conventional democracy is based on the rule of the majority. Deep democracy, in contrast, values the views of all actors on a stage, as well as their feelings and the atmosphere the stage and environment creates for everybody. Deep democracy is open to diversity and dialogue between various views and includes the awareness of rank and privileges, the diversity of communication styles, the role of the historical past and the vision for the future. It uses the three levels of awareness and observation framework described in chapter IV, which appreciates the need for practical consensus reality solutions (measurable objective descriptions of problems and people), as well as the support of subjective, non-measurable dreamlike and essence experiences. Deep democracy endorses the worldview of *Ubuntu,* which is an important and overarching worldview among the people of East, Central and Southern Africa. It captures the essence of what it means to be human. Simply explained, Ubuntu means "a person is a person through other people" (Tutu 1999). The concept of Ubuntu suggests that we are human because we live through others; our interdependence is such that our humanity is intertwined with the humanity of others. In its essence, Ubuntu means "I am you and you are me." Our separation is artificial and illusionary. By embracing Ubuntu and deep democracy ideas, individual and group facilitators focus not only on immediate practical goals but also on the information available from the deeper levels of our awareness. This invites more sustainable solutions and often creates spontaneous and surprising results.

A deep democracy approach to health addresses the practical needs of an individual, such as getting access to medical care, having the problems appropriately assessed and diagnosed and getting all treatment options, both allopathic and naturopathic or complementary. It also examines the individual lived experiences of an illness, the beliefs and values that surround and permeate the individual and his or her illness and the individual's innate wisdom that gives the whole experience meaning and direction. Generally speaking mainstream medicine regards the idea that illness can be a meaningful experience as superfluous at best, and possibly even vaguely subversive. For the mainstream, psychology is seen as playing a role in people's choices and behaviors rather than as a fundamental component of all body functions and processes. Mindell's original dreambody concept (1984), which I covered in the previous chapter, links the subjective non-measurable dreamlike experiences of illnesses to symbols, roles and patterns found in our night dreams, fantasies and other altered-state experiences. Using deep democracy and dreambody for examining individual health issues opens the door to potentially enriching experiences and to the discovery of extended meanings.

In addition, deep democracy is also a valuable way of thinking and method for taking care of community and public health matters. As we live and work within our communities, we interact with others and wander through a field and web of feelings, projections and some hurtful or disrespectful views. The explicit behaviors and implicit feelings, beliefs and projections have, as I described in chapter III, powerful effects on our bodies and the illnesses we experience.

Illness and suffering are a social experience: cultural values and collective modes of experience shape individual perceptions and expressions, and these culturally shaped patterns of how to bear with illness and disease are taught and learned via socialization. Social and family interactions influence sick people's illness experience. For example, the grief and pain of family members for their loved one with supposedly terminal cancer may limit the diseased to the terminal cancer patient role and co-create the negative outcome of the disease process. Negative expectations can be transmitted through health professionals' current health beliefs. They can have a great impact on patients' outcomes and chances for recovery.

This nocebo[45] effect is caused by the suggestion or belief that something is harmful. In the landmark epidemiological Framingham Heart study, women who believed they were prone to heart disease were nearly four times as likely to die as women with similar risk factors who didn't believe they were prone to these issues (Voelker 1996). Beliefs and expectations act like voodoo; they are strong medicine. Hope and hopelessness have direct effects on our bodies and our chances to recover. New drug treatments are introduced with a huge marketing and advertising effort. They get praised as the new solution for a certain disease, and doctors and the public alike are very excited about the new hope for this disease. Cultural hype is part of the beneficial effect of the new treatment. After a few years, when the treatment is not new and exciting anymore, the effect of the drug diminishes. Again, if we think of Ubuntu, we are all entangled and non-locally connected to each other. These non-local beliefs and projections are the foundation of our experience of community.

Thus, our individual processes and experiences are influenced by the characteristic cultural meanings of time and place and the ways we consciously and subconsciously communicate them to each other. These cultural beliefs and moral values mingle with the sick person's subjective experience and shape her ability to heal and recreate a renewed sense of self and a coherent view of her challenged life process.

Cultural spirits structure our communities. They give certain groups more privileges than others, they permit and deny access to resources, they define our gender roles and the power and rank assigned to certain roles, they grant people value and respect and demean others and they norm our thoughts and behaviors. The web of cultural values delimits the borders of mainstream and Consensus Reality (CR) and shape the level of inequity and disparities. Deep democracy methods are powerful in examining these processes and bringing them to the awareness of groups and communities. Deep democracy group work and open forums facilitate issues, facts and problems and addresses the non-local community field of feelings, beliefs and projections. These feelings, projections and beliefs are structured by roles, such as the oppressed and the oppressor, the healthy and the sick, the one with knowledge and

45 I will explain the nocebo effect in greater details in chapter VI.

expertise and the one that is helpless and out of control, etc. These roles are non-local, which means that we all share them to a certain degree; they can be found in just about everyone at one time or another. Deep democracy facilitators help people in these roles to communicate and dialogue with each other. They help them express their feelings and go deeper into the vision and meaning that they carry for the community. Deep democracy facilitation includes examining an individual illness experience in the midst of a community group and then exploring the roles that structure the individual process in a community dialogue. In such a dialogue one can unfold, for example, someone's process with a body image issue and uncover the roles of shamer and shamed. Both roles are widespread and can be processed in a larger community interaction. This, in turn, will help the individual feel less isolated with her body image problem.

## *Rank and Power Dynamics*

To facilitate deep democracy health dialogues, one needs to be aware of the roles that rank and power play in community relationship dynamics. From a public health perspective, inequality and the economic "gap" between the rich and the poor are the greatest health hazards. There are huge health differences that are caused by social and economic inequality, both within developed countries and between countries. Research on health disparities in developed countries shows that the average life expectancy is five, 10 or even 15 years shorter for people living in the poorest areas compared to those in the richest. And these health differences between the rich and the poor have increased in the last decades. Another health disparity regards individuals with serious mental illness. In the United States, they die on average 20 years earlier than the rest of the population.

The causal factor is relative poverty and not merely absolute poverty. The greater the disparity between the rich and the poor, the higher the difference gap is, and the poorer is the population's health. Studies are suggesting that relative poverty and processes of social comparison explain the high stress burden of individuals in countries with a big gap between the rich and the poor. This high stress is the biological pathway through which rank or hierarchy factors influence health. Income inequality is thought to create a sense of injustice and dissatisfaction, which is linked with a damaging state of physiological arousal and stress. Subjective feelings of humiliation, shame and resignation affect people's health. The process of social comparison, and the feelings we experience when we compare ourselves with the more privileged, affect our stress physiologies and immune systems. They contribute to the daily hassles and subtle put downs that raise our stress hormone levels and undermine our ability to fight bacteria, viruses and the cells that have become cancerous. Cultural and social dynamics are one important causal factor for ill health and early death.

Marmot's (1978) longitudinal epidemiological Whitehall study focused on 30,000 British civil servants, who work within a clear professional ranking system that allows correlating health outcomes with social rank. He uncovered an obvious gradient in mortality and morbidity from top to bottom of the social hierarchy. People further down the social ladder usually displayed at least twice the risk of serious illness and premature death as those near the top. The effects are not confined to the poor: the social gradient in health was shown to run right across society, so that even among middle-class office workers, lower-ranking staff suffered much more disease and earlier death than those in higher ranks.

These health disparities can be found in large systems and organizations; in communities, states and nations; and between whole countries. Despite spending the most money and resources in health care, the United States, for example, currently ranks 34th worldwide in life expectancy and mortality (United Nations Human Development Report 2011). It appears that with greater economic inequality comes worse health—lower life expectancy and higher mortality. Societies that distribute resources more equitably and have smaller gaps between the rich and poor fare better from a public health perspective and have better population health. Countries with a more cohesive social organization, such as Japan and some central and northern European countries, have better health statistics. All of the countries that rank higher in the so called "Health Olympics" have a smaller gap in income distribution between their richest and poorest citizens. One credible explanation is that the experience of relative poverty or low rank and the insult to personal dignity that it represents induce stress and have psychosomatic effects.

In a social context, there are many levels of influence and rank. On an individual level, there is personal dispositional power or rank, which is an individual's capacity to influence her own actions or those of others. That rank is either based on social categories such as gender, class, age, race, education and income, or it is based on psychological faculties grounded in personal development and awareness, or lastly it is based in spiritual or transpersonal power like one's connection to something larger than oneself, God, nature, etc.

Rank also depends on one's context or situation and derives from one's momentary roles in a given situation: as a teacher, health care provider, parent, bank teller, etc. Then there is systemic power and rank, which derives from the complex powerful forces that create situations and environments.

Our experience of rank has an impact on how we feel about ourselves and how much compassion we can have with ourselves. For most of us, our self-conception and self-esteem is dependent upon how others see us. William James described how our self-esteem depends on what we expect ourselves to be and do. It is determined by the difference between our actual achievements and supposed or envisioned potential. With every rise in our level of expectations comes the danger of failure and humiliation. Democracy and the pursuit of equal opportunities (in employment, education, in the face of disability, etc.) leveled the playing field for possibilities. It also increased the pressure of expectations and the perceived merit for successes and failures alike. De Botton remarks that "to the injury of poverty, a meritocratic system now added the insult of shame" (2004, 71). To be of low status is not only unfortunate but a failure. We are anxious about the place we occupy in the world because we intuitively know it determines how much love we receive and whether we can believe or lose confidence in ourselves.

In chapter III, we saw that biological normality, or health, is defined by a reference value from so called "healthy" individuals. Status and rank come from comparing ourselves to a reference group, a set of people who we believe are normal and resemble us. We see ourselves as fortunate and normal only when we abide by the standards of our peer group and community. Exposure to the presumed superior accomplishment of those whom we take to be our peers creates dissatisfaction and envy. The greater the achievement gap the bigger the sense of humiliation and worthlessness. Societies with a huge gap between the rich and poor instill in the ones that haven't been able to fulfill expectations shame, envy, resentment and bitterness. These feelings explain some of the health disparities between the more and less privileged.

Imagine the situation of one of my clients. She suffers from a genetic kidney disease that already killed her brother. She has been on dialysis for more than 25 years, is overweight, has chronic pain, lives in an adult foster care home and is chronically dependent and out of control. She feels vulnerable, irritable and angry and has many conflicts with her caregivers in her foster home. If we put ourselves in her "desolate" and difficult situation, we might understand her resentment toward anybody who is in relatively good health and has some control or power over her life. In my experience, being angry and irritable is a side effect of any chronic health condition, especially chronic pain. These emotions come with the disease. In addition, my client's anger is amplified by her lack of personal rank. To expect calmness and generosity of spirit shows how we don't understand chronic health problems and the role of rank in relationship interactions.

The experience of suffering from a chronic disease places you in a different culture. Imagine a white, healthy, mainstream woman who falls ill with a chronic disease such as Type II Diabetes. She is suddenly thrown into a new and marginalized race; she may suddenly understand a bit more what it is like to live as a person of color in a white culture (imagine what it means to be a person from a marginalized culture who also struggles with chronic health issues). She is now part of a minority and will experience all prejudices and negative consequences of being a minority individual. This I call healthism, which I define as the process of health prejudice and discrimination, a system of group privileges based on health and the unrecognized privileges and prejudices of healthy people toward their fellow human beings who suffer from chronic diseases. Healthism has all the characteristics of other isms, such as racism, sexism, ageism, etc. The healthy are the dominant, central culture and are unaware of the privileges they have in comparison to anybody who suffers from a chronic or serious disease. Being healthy gives you power and privilege in the same way as being a man, a white person or young.

Individual and cultural definitions of health have an effect on rank and power dynamics. A narrow definition of health that limits itself to the physical body, for instance, inherently marginalizes everybody who is dealing with chronic body problems. I am thankful to my colleague Nader Shabahangi (2010), the founder of AgeSong residential care communities, who alerted me to the fact that a body-centered definition of health excludes the elderly from feeling healthy. The biomedical decline model of aging focuses on the physical deterioration of an aging body. Its emphasis is based on pathology and the search for cures for age-related diseases. It derives its view principally from looking at aging and life from the outside and by emphasizing the material aspects of our bodies. This model marginalizes the value of spiritual strength, life review and meaning-of-life perspectives.

Rabbi Abraham Heschel said at a White House conference on aging in 1961:

> May I suggest that a person's potential for change and growth is much greater than we are willing to admit and that old age be regarded not as the age of stagnation but as the age of opportunities for inner growth. The old person must not be treated as a patient, nor should retirement be regarded as a prolonged state of resignation.

What this audacious spiritual man suggested is true for our elders and for anybody who is living with a physical disability or chronic health problem. He continues:

> Old age is a major challenge to the inner life; it takes both wisdom and strength not to succumb. According to all the standards we apply socially as well as privately, the aged person is condemned as inferior. In terms of manpower he is a liability, a burden, a drain on our resources. Conditioned to operate as a machine for making and spending money, with all other relationships dependent on its efficiency, the moment the machine is out of order and beyond repair, one begins to feel like a ghost without a sense of reality. The aged may be described as a person who does not dream anymore, devoid of ambition and living in fear of losing one's status. Regarded as a person who has outlived one's usefulness, one has to apologize for being alive.

You can replace the words old age and old person with sickness and ill person, and the message remains true. Health is much more than feeling well in your body. It's about feeling well emotionally, in relationships, feeling connected to the community and feeling well spiritually.

Healthism comes in many forms and is intertwined with biases about age, gender and physical and emotional disability. The focus on pathology and decline permeates much of our culture and contributes to upholding a certain image of the body as more desirable than another. It isolates our elders and people with disabilities. This is absurd because "disability," "decline" and aging are common experiences, and all of us at some point in our lives will experience limited functionality. Projects like Sins Invalid: An Unashamed Claim to Beauty in the Face of Invisibility[46] help us reclaim the diversity of our bodies and the shared beauty of our vulnerabilities.

Knowing and acknowledging rank differences allows us to improve some caregiver-patient relationship conflicts. Understanding how our health beliefs impact others facilitates communication, creates trust and gives sick people the sense of being seen and heard. In addition, helping individuals with chronic health issues increase their rank, sense of empowerment and control can help diffuse some of the conflicts. Like healthism, ableism is the bias against persons with disabilities. For people who have not yet experienced disability, we are only temporarily able bodied (TAB); as people who have not yet experienced illness, we are only temporarily healthy bodied (THB). As caregivers and health professionals, we can keep this in mind and treat our patients with the knowledge that sooner or later we will be in their place.

Health care providers experience "healthism" in a different way. For them, healthism represents a particular way of viewing health problems and is characteristic of the new health consciousness and related movements. Some health care providers complain that people pay excessive attention to their own health. With easy access to information, high expectations, a distrust of doctors and critical views on science, health-aware middle-class individuals express anxiety; demand more tests; are concerned about unnatural substances, toxins and vaccines; and fear small insidious threats, such as leaky gut syndrome, amalgam tooth fillings, etc. Some researcher argue that the very success of medicine in addressing disease has raised expectations for its far less successful attempts to influence subjective health, well-being and quality of life. Crawford (1980, 365) states that "by elevating health to a super

46 See bibliography for a link to the group's web page.

value, a metaphor for all that is good in life, healthism reinforces the privatization of the struggle for generalized well-being."

## CULTURAL COMPETENCY

Rank awareness, knowledge of social and relational dynamics and understanding how our beliefs and biases have an effect on relationships are components of cultural competency. What is cultural competency? It is a set of behaviors, attitudes and policies that come together in a system, agency or group of providers that enables effective work in cross-cultural situations. "Culture" refers to integrated patterns of human behavior that include the language, thoughts, communications, actions, customs, beliefs, values and institutions of racial, ethnic, religious or social groups. "Competence" implies having the capacity to function effectively as an individual and an organization within the context of the cultural beliefs, behaviors and needs presented by individuals and their communities (adapted from Cross 1989).

This definition of culture applies also to various illness cultures[47]. Illness experiences that last a certain time develop into integrated behavioral patterns with specific thoughts, beliefs and values. Commonly, we tend to see culture as based on ethnicity and we fail to acknowledge cultural differences in terms of age, gender, sexual orientation and health.

Why is cultural competency important? It is a valuable element in addressing health disparities. It allows patients and doctors to come together and communicate without cultural barriers hindering the conversation. Quite simply, culturally competent services bring about positive health outcomes. Cultural competency requires knowledge but even more so awareness. Culture acts like blinders that narrow our field of vision. Like rank, we are often not aware of our cultural biases, which act like blind spots or scotomas[48]. We look at the world through our own limited set of values, which influences our relationship with patients and health care providers from other cultures. Knowledge

---

47 See also chapter VII.

48 A scotoma (Greek for darkness) is an area of partial alteration in the field of vision consisting of a partially diminished or entirely degenerated visual acuity that is surrounded by a field of normal or relatively well-preserved vision.

helps us broaden our understanding of other cultures, but it is impossible to know everything about someone else's culture.

When I started working as a counselor in the Unites States as a newly arrived immigrant from Switzerland, some of my clients expressed general dissatisfaction with me. Initially, I didn't understand until one client told me she was confused because I didn't look her in the eyes. She said she felt disrespected. Growing up in Switzerland, I was never taught to look into people's eyes; on the contrary, it seems slightly invasive to Swiss people. I had to learn this and I explain now to new clients that it is not in my nature and culture to look into people's eyes directly. I tell them that when I look down, it allows me to stay connected with myself while I listen to them. There are many even more subtle cultural details that are impossible to learn. This is why we need cultural awareness, a sensitivity to cultural issues that allows us to be open and interested in other people's cultures.

The increasing ethnic diversity of the population, plus other cultural characteristics (gender, age, health status, sexual orientation, etc.) pose a challenge to all of us. We bring our learned patterns of language and culture to the health care experience, which we must transcended to improve our communication and develop a good alliance and relationship.

Culture helps determine our thoughts, communications, actions, customs, beliefs and values. Culture stems from the land, geography and culture we grew up in; the family beliefs and values that our parents instilled in us; and the peer cultures of our gender and sexual orientation. It influences our health, healing and wellness belief systems; how we perceive illness, disease and their causes; how we express our problems and symptoms; and our relationships.

In sum, because health and health care are cultural constructs, arising from beliefs about the nature of disease and the human body, cultural issues are actually central in the delivery of services and compliance with treatment and preventive interventions. Cultural competency starts with being open about our own diversity. Having a rigid notion of who we are and marginalizing our inner diversity is the first barrier to interpersonal cultural competency. Paradoxically, our own illness experiences give us an opportunity to broaden our personal cultural competency. We need to be candid about our individual beliefs and values—how they benefit and limit us. A good way to develop our cultural competency is to use irritations and frustration about our own or someone else's behavior to examine diversity and the barriers to inner and outer openness to diversity[49].

Besides social disparities, community biases and stereotypes (i.e., healthism) and our intra- and inter-personal cultural competency, there are other systemic and structural factors that influence health and health care. Body systems are nested within other larger systems such as food systems, farming systems, manufacturing systems, etc. The US Farm Bill, for example, subsidizes certain crop insurances (i.e., corn and soy), which plays a part in the dissemination of these products in our diets. The Toxic Substances Control Act hasn't been updated since its inception in 1976, which allows for the widespread use of toxic organophosphate pesticides in agriculture. Human health, public health and ecological health are entangled and require interventions at the community and policy levels. Knowledge of these matters helps us take care of health in its community and social context, see the individual as part of the sociobiological system and facilitate awareness and dialogue. From a global perspective, we can then recognize the value of health as a human rights issue.

## *Health—a Human Right*

When thinking of health as a human rights issue, a story comes to mind of two Iraqi refugee women, a mother and a grandmother. Both were newly arrived in Portland and were referred to me because at their initial health screening they reported significant post-traumatic distress. Both had experienced loss when their husbands passed away from diabetes and heart attack. Both women suffered from high blood pressure, diabetes and heart problems themselves. They couldn't sleep and were haunted by terrible memories and nightmares.

Their health problems are normal reactions to pathological circumstances. Their health is as much an individual problem as a community issue, a cultural issue and a human rights problem. Staying healthy in such circumstances would be abnormal. As we discussed earlier, health is both individual and collective. Public health is related to social, economic and human rights or the lack thereof. Social and economic inequalities are major contributors to poor health and early death. The

49 See exercise in appendix II toolkit.

stress of injustice, poverty and war makes whole communities sick and ends up killing them. Today, we handle human rights and social justice issues through declarations, treaties and international laws. But these human and social dynamics are also embedded in day-to-day community relationships and governed by group and field dynamics. Laws and conventions are necessary but alone are insufficient in resolving equality and diversity issues. Community-based approaches help process the conflicts between polarized roles and help raise awareness about their meaning. Equity and democracy need to be complemented with a processing of roles and the feelings that social dynamics evoke.

Extremely stated, you can kill a dictator like Hosni Mubarak, Saddam Hussein or Osama Bin Laden, but you can't kill the role. A role will resurge in different clothes, as in Egypt with the military or the Islamist president Mohamed Morsi from the Muslim Brotherhood. You can implement so called "upstream" interventions that give people access to more resources, health care, healthy foods, etc., but you can't get rid of the role of the one who profits and abuses privileges. Group process, open forums and other community-based dialogues and interventions are needed to engage us all in creating a new community that cares about the health and contributions of all its members.

An enumeration of public health risks include: stress, trauma, adverse childhood events, inequality and inequity, social marginalization, poverty, war, rank and power abuse, race- and gender-based discrimination, sexual and domestic violence, addictions and many more. If unprocessed, they pose the biggest health challenge. Injustice in itself is obviously problematic and needs to be corrected. Inequality is also an aspect of diversity, which allows for awareness. Without diversity there is no consciousness. The problem lies in the lack of community processing of feelings that are attached to the diversity issues. What is missing is a culture of bringing the roles into the same room, helping them relate with each other and facilitating the sharing of views and beliefs they carry; this benefits the entire community.

Health means life and health means freedom, and both life and freedom are moral issues. If you get a major illness or injury and cannot get it treated adequately, you could die. And tens of thousands do. In 2010, 16.3% of the US population or 49.9 million people remained without health insurance and researchers from Harvard Medical School tied the lack of coverage to about 45,000 deaths a year (Wilper 2009). If you have a serious illness or injury and cannot get it treated, your freedom and human rights will be limited in many ways. Consider the impacts on your physical freedom: you may no longer have the freedom to move around. Your economic freedom: you may not be able to work or your medical bills may impoverish you. Your emotional freedom: you may not be free to live a happy life. Health is, therefore, a moral issue of the highest order. In many countries, health security and access to appropriate care is a far bigger concern than military security. An individual's security is far more likely to be threatened by the lack of treatment for illness and injury than by any potential terrorist attack.

Health is one of the most pressing social justice issues. From a human rights perspective, we need health security, open access to the right care, a more equitable distribution of economic and educational resources and culturally competent care. For lasting benefits and sustainability we also need to create community spaces where the roles of the abuser, perpetrator, competitor, privileged, etc., can be processed. They are here to teach us, also.

How do these systemic factors impact an individual's health? What are the mechanisms that cause the body to collapse under the attack of social stress, and what resources does the body have to fend off the attacks? I will explore these questions in the next chapter using placebo and nocebo pathways as examples.

6

# *Enhancing Placebo and Preventing Nocebo: The Biology of Hope and Despair*

In this chapter, I explore placebo and nocebo[50] reactions as exemplary processes for all relevant mind-body connections. I go over the relevant scientific stress theories and how stress and trauma affects our physiologies. This knowledge allows us to boost our self-healing powers.

Imagine sucking the juice of a tart lemon. Notice your body reaction. Probably 100 percent of us reacted with some salivation. A simple thought incites a series of physiological reactions that produce saliva: this is at the core of the placebo or nocebo effect and the mind-body connection—and we have yet to explain how this works.

We know it is linked to classical conditioning or associative learning, the process by which a behavior and stimulus or two stimuli are connected. It means that, by experience, you have learned to associate the taste of lemon with producing saliva. This leads us to produce the same reaction merely by thinking about it or seeing an image that triggers that association. But how exactly that translation process from an immaterial thought to a physical reaction occurs, nobody knows.

---

50 Nocebo reactions are the harmful side effects of medical practices and drug treatments that are not directly linked to the treatments and practices themselves but to the negative suggestions and expectations that are associated with them.

## *Placebo*

Placebo stems from the Latin verb "placere" to please. The medical usage of a placebo was first recorded in 1785 in a statement that described: "a medicine given more to please than to benefit the patient." (Shapiro 1968) Historically in medieval times, rich citizens hired "fake" mourners or grief simulators to recite the 114 psalm in the Office of the Dead church service: "placebo Domino in regione vivorum" or "I will please the Lord in the land of the living." Often, singers of placebo falsely claimed a connection to the deceased to get a share of the funeral meal. This deceptive act to please is why placebo is still connected with fakeness and simulators.

Placebos were common in medicine until the 20th century; they were sometimes approved as necessary deception and used as dud substances for malingerers and hypochondriacs. Later they were introduced in randomized control studies to separate the "verum" or physiological effect of a drug from other non-drug-related outcomes.

Placebo effects are thought to rely on the effects of medical rituals and the provider-patient relationship. They have to be differentiated from natural fluctuations, spontaneous remissions, statistical "errors" (regression to the mean) and beneficial physical co-occurring interventions such as changes in rest, diet and exercise patterns. The placebo effect is the difference between the placebo response and the changes that would be observed even without the administration of a placebo, such as natural fluctuations and spontaneous remissions.

In other words, placebo is a substance containing no medication and prescribed or given to reinforce a patient's expectation to get well. It is also used to describe an inactive substance or preparation used as a control in an experiment or test to determine the effectiveness of a medicinal drug. Further, placebo stands for the healing that arises from medical ritual, the relationship between provider and patient, the context of treatment and the power of imagination, trust and hope. Placebo describes the significant healing that results from the belief and expectation that you have received a powerful remedy, even if you were actually given a sugar pill, saline water, or sham surgery.

## *Nocebo*

Nocebo is Latin for: "I will be harmful." It was first used to describe the experienced side effects of placebos. People enrolled in drug studies and unknowingly receiving the placebo treatment described symptoms they assigned to the harmless placebo substance or procedure. They usually mirror the "verum" drug side effects. Nocebo effects come from suggestions and expectations, the instruction from the provider, the therapeutic milieu and the psychological condition or anxiety of the patient.

Informing a patient, for example, that a prescribed drug or procedure causes a side effect may produce the same side effect. Nicola Mondaini (2007) demonstrated that the disclosure of possible sexual side effects from a drug treating benign prostate tumors increased the probability of these effects.

While an inert sugar pill (placebo) can make you feel better, warnings of fictional side effects (nocebo) can make you feel those, too. Therefore, it is known that patients are far more likely to suffer side effects from their medical treatments if they have first been warned of those side effects. This poses an ethical quandary: should doctors warn patients about side effects if doing so makes them more likely to arise? In our current medical environment, health professionals are trained to disclose all drug side effects and inform patients about the possible dangers of any medical procedures and treatments. This is based on a basic sense of decency and caring as well as on fears of litigation and other legal issues. As health care providers, we are taught to convey realistic expectations, discourage false hopes and get the patients' informed consent. The pharmacy drug pamphlets and TV advertisements explicitly enumerate all possible side effects. That culture contributes to the adverse symptoms that people experience.

Nocebo can also play a role in individuals who undergo cancer treatment. They will often begin experiencing side effects that are widely known about, such as nausea, before their first round of chemotherapy. If they later get into a room that is painted the same color of the room where they've gotten chemotherapy treatment, they will feel nauseated. If you show someone who is allergic some inert dust in a concealed container or a fake plastic rose, you can create an allergic reaction. If I make you think of sucking on a lemon, you will immediately experience some salivation.

In general, if you, your environment and your caregivers believe in a certain treatment, the outcomes will be more positive; if you are convinced of the opposite, you might experience more side effects or even harm from the treatment. Placebo and nocebo effects clearly show that brain activities can be steered by one's mental beliefs and expectations and that those mental processes are translated into neural brain events.

In the previous chapter, I showed how non-material or psychological processes have a huge impact on our bodies. Difficult life circumstances change our ability to stay healthy. The experience of poverty, marginalization, trauma, abuse and adverse childhood events increase our susceptibility to developing diseases like cancer, heart problems and many others. If the daily hassles of socio-cultural circumstances are too challenging, the body will experience some wear and tear due to over-stimulation of its stress responses. The stresses that can break down our defenses are multiple. They can start when we are still in the womb and continue through infancy and adulthood. They include marginalization, fear, trauma and abuse, as well as ongoing feelings of not being good enough and having low self-esteem.

On the other hand, there is comparable evidence that positive feelings of warmth, hope, humorous detachment, trust, friendship, community, prayer and a spiritual connection of some sort have positive health effects. In that vein, placebo and nocebo are examples of psychologically or emotionally mediated health effects.

Images, thoughts and nonverbal clues from the environment and providers have a non-local effect on physical bodies. Beliefs, attitudes, hopes and fears are transmitted non-locally and affect individual health outcomes. The renowned cardiologist Bernhard Lown provides many examples of the extraordinary power of words—words that transcend the mechanical body, those that injure and maim us and those that heal. One dazzling example is the case of a 60-year-old, critically ill man who recovered after he heard Dr. Lown refer to the galloping sound of his heart, which is paradoxically a bad prognostic sign in conditions of heart failure.

> On Thursday morning, April twenty-fifth, you came in with your gang, surrounded the bed, and looked as though I was already in the casket. You put your stethoscope on my chest and urged everyone to listen to the "wholesome gallop." I figured that if my

heart was still capable of a healthy gallop, I couldn't be dying, and I got well. (1999, 82)

From a materialist point of view, placebo and nocebo effects don't make sense. Materialism is unable to explain how immaterial mental thoughts and feelings translate into biophysical and chemical processes. Classical Newtonian physics can't explain how subjective experiences or psychology influence our material bodies, but quantum mechanics, as we have seen in chapter III, opens the door for a unifying theory of a *bodymind*.

From a bodymind perspective, the findings from placebo studies mean that encouragement, support and hope are essential ingredients of any therapy. Nocebo effects demonstrate that implicit and explicit expectations can also have harmful consequences. Overall, psychology and field forces, the way we process issues individually and collectively and thoughts and feelings are a crucial part of medicine and healing.

Until recently, we knew very little about how placebo and nocebo effects worked. Now, however, a number of scientists are beginning to make headway. Current medical understandings of how subjective experiences are translated into physiology are based on findings from mind-body medicine and our knowledge of the functioning of the human brain and mind. It's in the mind and the brain that healing, psychology, culture and environment intertwine. Individual brains and minds, together with their endocrine and immune systems, are nested within the larger sociocultural, political and ecological systems. The placebo and nocebo effects are examples of the interaction of these systems. It is this psycho-neuro-immuno-endocrinology system that provides the machinery of stress and coping with stress or healing. The mind produces brain states that send their own signals to immune cells and hormonal glands. Hormones and nerve chemicals then tune up or down the immune cells' ability to fight disease.

## *Stress Response*

The body's reaction to stress, or stress response, is determined by the interplay of these physiological systems. Recent scientific advances in psychology, neurology, immunology and endocrinology have led to a clearer understanding of the connection among these systems, revealing possible mechanisms by which the body responds to environmental and social stress.

Neurons are the fundamental cellular communication unit of the nervous system. They communicate with each other by producing chemical substances called neurotransmitters, which are sent across synapses between the neurons (Kalat 2001). The action of these neurotransmitters (e.g., serotonin) is the basis for brain functioning. These chemicals have been linked to behaviors as diverse as learning and memory, motor activity, thirst, pain, thermo-regulation, pleasure, stress, emotions, mood and sexual receptivity.

The two main organ sites for this "biological embedding" (Hertzman 1999) of human experience are the autonomic nervous system and the hypothalamic-pituitary-adrenal (HPA) axis. Together, they mediate our adaptive response to stress by first initiating an increase in circulating catecholamines (e.g., adrenaline or epinephrine) and glucocorticoids (e.g., cortisol), which alter the structure and function of a variety of cells and tissues. When a threat to our physical or psychological well-being is detected, the hypothalamus amplifies the production of corticotropin-releasing factor (CRH), which induces the pituitary to secrete adrenocorticotropic hormone (ACTH), which then instructs the adrenal gland atop each kidney to release cortisol. Together, these changes prepare our bodies to fight or flee and shut down activities that would distract us from self-protection. For instance, cortisol enhances the delivery of fuel to our muscles. At the same time, CRH depresses our appetite for both food and sex and heightens our alertness. Chronic activation of the HPA axis, however, may lay the ground for illness. For each organ system of the body, these stress mediators have both short-term adaptive and protective and long-term damaging effects if the stress response is overextended. Examples of harmful reactions are: increase of heart rate and blood pressure, augmented risk of atherosclerosis and Type II diabetes, cognitive dysfunction and increased risks of autoimmune and inflammatory disorders.

Life course factors interact with our contemporary circumstances both on a moment-by-moment basis and over time. The systematic differences in the quality of our environments and life paths shape the sculpting and neurochemistry of our central nervous systems. Animal studies have shown that the immune system can be conditioned by outer events. Ader and Cohen (1984) convincingly demonstrate how conditioned learning can directly influence the competence of our immune system. They treated mice with the immune disease lupus with cyclophosphamide, a drug that suppresses the immune system. As expected, the mice improved. They then conditioned the mice to associate saccharine-sweetened water with cyclophosphamide and were able to reproduce the same improvement by giving the mice a sweetened placebo solution. This experiment showed that the immune system, like other physiological systems, can be trained to respond to the process of associative learning.

Moreover, the observation that the immune system can be conditioned implies that these effects can endure beyond the precipitating event. Thus, the mind and brain, which interpret the environment, can also influence the long-term functions of the immune, hormonal and blood clotting systems.

Two new terms have been used to describe these physiological stress responses: "allostasis," for the adaptive maintenance of stability through change and "allostatic load," for the wear and tear the body experiences due to overstimulation of allostatic cycles (McEwen and Seeman 1999). Our individual allostatic load represents the biological signature of our cumulative psychosocial experience of adversity. Various physiologic parameters (e.g., systolic and diastolic blood pressure, waist-hip ratio, serum HDL, total cholesterol and overnight urinary cortisol excretion) have been investigated as measures of allostatic load.

Similar to the damaging stress response, the body's psycho-neuro-immuno-endocrinology system mediates the positive belief response or the health promoting changes. Studies of placebo effects, meditation, prayer and miracle cures in Lourdes, France, have shown these experiences to induce specific brain states that stimulate massive activation of the dopamine reward pathways or opioid pain pathways in the brain, which in turn trigger a release of the anti-inflammatory hormone cortisol and/or endorphins into the bloodstream. At the same time, adrenaline-like nerve chemicals (norepinephrine) are released into the spleen and other immune organs and change the immune-cell functions. Together, these hormones and nerve chemicals have profound and rapid effects on alleviating pain, lifting mood, facilitating movement and reducing inflammation. In one such study at the University of California, San Francisco, Jon Levine and Howard Fields (1978) gave patients either morphine, naloxone (a drug that would block the body's own opioids or endorphins) or a placebo saline solution following the extraction of impacted wisdom teeth. Pain was reduced in the patients who received morphine, and also those who believed they were receiving morphine but who received only placebo saline. Patients who received the endorphin-blocking drug naloxone felt much more pain than patients in other groups. These studies clearly showed that the placebo effect has a biological basis. Other hormones and nerve chemicals that play a role in the stress and belief responses include estrogen, progesterone, oxytocin, vasopressin and prolactin.

A study by Irene Tracey in Oxford (2010) showed that when study participants felt nocebo pain, corresponding brain activities were detectable in a brain scanner. This showed that, at the neurological level at least, these participants were responding to actual, non-imaginary pain. Fabrizio Benedetti (2006), of the University of Turin, and his colleagues have managed to determine one of the neurochemicals responsible for converting the expectation of pain into this genuine pain perception. The chemical, called cholecystokinin, is responsible for carrying messages between nerve cells. When drugs are used to block cholecystokinin from functioning, patients feel no nocebo pain, despite being just as anxious.

The findings of Benedetti and Tracey not only offer first glimpses into the neurology underlying the nocebo effect, but they also have very real medical implications. Benedetti and colleagues were able to antagonize the pain effect of cholecystokinin with anti-anxiety medication such as diazepam or valium. Treating anxiety could pave the way for techniques that remove nocebo outcomes from medical procedures. The findings of Tracey's team carry startling implications for the way we practice modern medicine. They found that telling a study participant who had received strong pain medication that the drug had worn off was enough for his or her pain to return to the levels it was at before the drug was administered. This indicates that individuals' negative expectations have the power to undermine the effectiveness of a treatment and suggests that doctors would do well to treat the beliefs of their patients—not just their physical symptoms.

A person's genetic makeup in terms of dopamine metabolism may explain some of the variances in the placebo effect (Hall 2012). Dopamine, which plays important roles in the brain system, is responsible for reward-driven learning, for responses to stimulants and other addictive substances and for modulating pain perception. Genetically driven differences in the way dopamine is cleared in the neural synapses may explain why some people are more sensitive to placebos and nocebos than others. Existing studies have looked at general unspecific effects. Scientists are just beginning to explore more specific effects and to study how providers can enhance placebo and prevent nocebo effects. The main focus is on the provider-patient relationship, as it is perceived as the one interaction or mechanism that gives the "biggest bang for the buck." Behaviors such as bestowing warmth and compassion, active empathic listening and reflecting back are thought to enhance the placebo effect. New ways of informing patients and providing instructions may prevent negative side effects, or nocebos. Today's society is litigious and skeptical, and if doctors overemphasize side effects to their patients in order to avoid being sued, or patients mistrust their doctor's chosen course of action, the nocebo effect can cause a treatment to fail before it has begun. It also introduces a paradox—we must believe in our providers if we are to gain the full benefits of their prescribed treatments; but if we trust in them completely, we can be harmed from their pronouncements. In the book *Inside Coma,* for example, Gary Reiss and I (2010) described how caregivers' lack of hope influences comatose patients' chance to regain consciousness and recover.

To my knowledge, nobody has studied how an individual's emotional and psychological processes stimulate his or her belief response. Mindell's dreambody and deep democracy concepts open the door for studying and providing individualized treatment approaches that enhance our bodies' self-healing or placebo effects.

## *Enhancing the Placebo Effect*

The power of the patient-provider interaction to enhance healing is one of the hallmarks of clinical medicine, and increasingly, resources are devoted to teaching clinicians how to communicate warmth, caring and hope to their patients. Placebo effects do not require placebos. That is because even active medical treatments have placebo components. The response to an effective medical treatment is made up of various components. These include a treatment effect (the treatment response minus the placebo response), a placebo effect (the difference between the placebo response and no treatment at all) and the natural progression of the disease. Because placebo and drug effects are usually additive, enhancing the placebo component of treatment can enhance the treatment response. The question then becomes, how can we enhance the placebo component of a medical treatment? One answer is to spend more time with the patient and take more care to form a therapeutic alliance. But this goes against current medical cultures and practices, where in general most providers are pressed for time. Typically, primary care doctors have about 10 minutes to devote to a patient during a visit. They just do not have the time to foster a solid therapeutic relationship. As a consequence, this constriction may have a cost in terms of treatment outcome. It also means we need to find additional ways to foster our patients' self-healing capacities, or placebo responses.

As health care professionals, we want to think our knowledge, expertise, skills, interventions and prescriptions are what heal people. On the other hand, people's behavior (e.g., their compliance with treatment directions) is relevant to the outcomes. It is significant then, that in the US more than 30 percent of doctors' prescriptions are not followed and yet some people get well regardless. Others who do follow their doctor's prescriptions and live a healthy lifestyle may nevertheless get or remain sick. Health and sickness is complex, and we will probably never fully understand the causal connections.

Obviously, modern medicine has made much progress, and many of us are now able to live longer, healthier lives because of the progress made. But again, as discussed above, psychology and individual and collective emotional intelligence (EQ) have a significant influence on people's health and ability to heal. Social circumstances such as education, money, access to individual power and other resources, the stress of war and social marginalization are other important factors. What is health and what promotes or hinders healing is complex, and many intertwined factors contribute to the outcome. Health itself is a difficult and complex concept with probably as many definitions as there are people on this planet. In healing, there are many intangible factors that elude us.

I have found Mindell's description of the three levels of experience[51] helpful to frame the complexity of our lived body experiences and to give us some orientation. On a consensus reality level, our health is

51 These are described in depth in chapter IV.

determined by mechanistic and material determinants (e.g., the level of health professionals' hard skills and knowledge, clients' behaviors and social dynamics). On the dreaming level, there are psycho-emotional and relational processes that determine the course of a disease process. And on the sentient level, we are all spiritually whole, no matter what, sick or well.

Let me give you an example from my own experience. About four years after immigrating to the United States, I became sick. I was having diffuse abdominal pains that came and went without a recognizable pattern. I was under considerable stress finishing the dissertation for my PhD, working as an underpaid mental health counselor and going through the difficult process of applying for permanent residency in the US. I treated myself for possible stomach ulcers without much success. One night, the pain was so intensive that I had to go to the ER. There, the doctors quickly diagnosed me with having gall stones and an inflamed gall bladder. They recommended immediate surgery, which they performed very well. But after the surgery my blood markers didn't return to normal levels. Through the intermediary of nurses, doctors recommended a second surgical intervention to release some blockage they assumed was remaining. The surgeon didn't have time to come and explain the situation to me in person. I remember lying in bed, and because of my own training, I knew a lot about the medical process, but I still felt anxious and increasingly frustrated about the lack of communication between my doctors and myself. I then remembered a dream I'd had the night before. It was of a big cathedral with a small chimney that was blowing off steam under a lot of pressure. Over the phone, a friend helped me work on that dream and got me in contact with my own anger about the lack of appropriate communication. I also got back in touch with my own core beliefs and values and felt re-empowered.

Later that evening, a nurse told me the doctors had decided to check my blood levels again before making a final decision about surgery. I would need to remain on an IV and without food in order to be ready for surgery. In the middle of the night, my IV got blocked and needed to be replaced. I still felt hopeful about my chances of not needing the second surgical procedure, and so I asked if they could wait before giving me another IV. The poor nurse had to go back and forth communicating with me and the doctor on night duty. I got so fed up that

I asked for the doctor to come in person to explain his reasoning. I told the nurse I wouldn't have her do anything to me before I was able to talk to the doctor myself. The poor resident on night duty had to pay for the lack of overall communication between the doctors and me, but after another hour he came and we had a good chat. I agreed to get another IV, despite the fact that I thought it might not be necessary. The most intriguing part of the process was that after all the emotional processing, my body reacted by letting go of built-up fluids and internal pressure. In the morning, they took my blood and everything was back to normal. I was discharged the same morning without further surgery.

What healed me and prevented the second surgery? How were my anger and frustration connected to the temporary blockage? How was my insistence on fair treatment and communication related to my letting go of the buildup of water in my body? Did the reduction in interstitial fluids reduce some swelling that had been contributing to some blockage? I also remember that on the phone I had been able to process some deep feelings I was having about my current experience in the United States. The US laws and regulations hadn't accepted my Swiss medical training and didn't allow me to practice as a medical doctor, which was humiliating. As an alternative to returning to medical school, I had chosen to do a second training in health psychology. This had forced me to start at the bottom again. The lack of communication with the doctors had reinforced my sense of not being recognized and respected as a colleague. I was feeling low, not only because of being sick but also about my experience of not being validated for my medical knowledge and experience.

The whole process taught me there are many factors that contribute to healing, which go beyond hard medical skills and technical interventions. In my case, the surgery was necessary and professionally executed. But then my healing was also embedded in a relevant personal psychological and emotional context. Both medicine and psychology have a lot to add to healing. Psychology allows us to access the body's innate healing powers: facilitating the body's dreaming process and the emotional dynamics between the parties involved in the healing process are powerful tools that complement and enhance the effectiveness of medical interventions. Healing is a combination of consensus reality medical interventions, alternative medical interventions, the individual's awareness process and the way nature moves this process.

As providers and patients, we share the responsibility to improve our bodies' self-healing capacities. As providers we need to take more time, learn to listen, learn to instill hope and take care of the relationship with our patients. Deep and empathic listening might also include the ability to listen to the dreaming story that the body is trying to express. In a process oriented treatment, one can imagine a provider asking her patient about a night dream and taking a few minutes to wonder together how the dream might be connected to the illness process. We are well trained to ask our patients about their level of pain. How about asking about the quality of the pain and relating the specific pain experience to the patient's overall life situation? If there is pressure: who and what is pressuring our patient, and what stops him or her from retorting? Being curious about our patients' inner experiences, finding ways to help them examine them and express them creatively could go a long way toward improving our relationships and supporting their self-healing capacities. As Antonovsky (1979) and Frankl (2006) have shown us, resilience has to do with one's ability to maintain a sense of coherence, stay in touch with our purpose and meaning in life and foster good relationships.

As patients, even though we have less rank and are dependent on our providers, we share some responsibility to care for the relationship. Knowing that the alliance with our providers is some of the most powerful medicine, we definitively benefit from doing what we can to improve our relationship with them. We need to help them help us. We can share our expectations and hopes and take some time to discuss with them how to support the relationship and smaller communities. Historically primary care providers have and continue to be an intrinsic part of the fabric of the community. Today, most providers and patients won't share the same communal space. We need to help recreate that as part of our own treatment plans. As patients, we also need to take care of our care teams and families. They are part of the healing environment and can contribute to our own self-healing. Mindfulness and prayer circles have non-local effects on our bodies. Bringing awareness to the community about our health issues and facilitating dialogues that examine the collective aspects of our health is another way we can support our own and others' healing. Lastly, in the book's toolkit located in appendix II, I describe some brief "exercises" we all can do individually and together to increase our understanding of our own mind-body connection and the stories that our bodies are telling.

## Enhancing Placebo from a Community Perspective

As we have seen, self-healing powers are embedded in community values, beliefs and expectations. They are also influenced by power and rank dynamics and the exclusion from social and economic resources. As individuals, we live in a community field that exhibits powerful forces. Physical and subjective healing requires individual and collective approaches. Focusing on the individual omits the significant, larger social and economic justice issues. If we are serious about health and equity, we need to support efforts that bring community and public health issues into public awareness. I am currently working with someone on an individual health problem in front of a group and using the outcome of the individual work to lead into a group process that explores the various roles expressed in the individual work. Similarly, hospital patients could benefit from an internal TV broadcast that would air someone's health and illness process. These efforts will help reduce the shame and isolation many sick people experience. They will foster support groups and individual resilience, a collective attitude of togetherness, interconnectedness and Ubuntu. They will expand our diversity awareness to include the multiple illness lands and cultures[52]. They will increase the rank awareness of normotypicals[53], benefit everybody and lead to a new understanding of sustainable health, which includes sickness.

There are many interest groups and systemic forces that influence health policy changes. Many parties and advocacy groups will promote certain policies to benefit their constituents. These efforts are important. I would also encourage communities to be more creative and create spaces where we can come together and share our experiences and learning. Community provider dialogues are an invaluable place for cultural competency learning. They provide the forum to learn from each other, build community and foster relationships. Open forums are another venue to address collective issues. Many times action teams will emerge and collaborate for change.

---

52 See chapter VII.

53 Ibid.

## *Conclusion*

As Kenneth Pelletier (1993, 19) puts it:

> Asthmatics sneeze at plastic flowers. People with a terminal illness stay alive until after a significant event, apparently willing themselves to live until a graduation ceremony, a birthday milestone, or a religious holiday. A bout of rage precipitates a sudden, fatal heart attack. Specially trained people can voluntarily control such 'involuntary' bodily functions as the electrical activity of the brain, heart rate, bleeding, and even the body's response to infection. Mind and body are inextricably linked, and their second-by-second interaction exerts a profound influence upon health and illness, life and death. Attitudes, beliefs, and emotional states ranging from love and compassion to fear and anger can trigger chain reactions that effect blood chemistry, heart rate, and the activity of every cell and organ system in the body. All of that is now indisputable fact. However, there is still great debate over the extent to which the mind can influence the body and the precise nature of that linkage.

Today, many of the fastest-growing illnesses are relatively new and characterized solely by a collection of complaints. Allergies, food intolerances and back pain could easily be real, physiological illnesses in some and nocebo-induced conditions in others. Pelletier's example illustrates how, more than a century ago, doctors found they could induce a hay fever sufferer's wheezing by exposure to an artificial rose. Observations like these suggest we should think about ways to reinforce placebo and minimize nocebo effects. The best ways to do this is by strengthening our relationships and develop more understanding about the individual and community dreaming processes that express themselves through our individual and collective bodies. Process oriented mindfulness exercises and community dialogues are a step in that direction.

7

## *Health-In-Sickness and Sickness-In-Health*

In this chapter I bring the various theories and examples into a cohesive framework that accepts the diversity of health and sickness and illustrates the dangers of a narrow health orientation.

### *Health-in-Sickness*

People who are dealing with illness are not just sick. Even when they face life-threatening diseases, the illness is only one aspect of their lives. As we have seen, the illness process has many health ingredients. In my experience, most people hate to be one-sidedly identified with their illness process. Addressing them with too much concern can be patronizing and dismaying, even when well intended. As Susan Halpern says in her book *The Etiquette of Illness*: "The minor key does not sit well with people who are trying to be hopeful. As a sick person, I don't want to be responsible for cheering you up" (2004, 18). The disease is part of a person's wholeness. It is not only something that needs to be fixed and cured. The current medical model, with its definitions of pathology and what is not normal, has allowed for immense progress in treating and curing disease. I am very thankful for the knowledge, tools and therapies that are available for so many of us, and I am all for more advancement in medicine. In addition, I hope to contribute to a change in attitude that is inquisitive and curious about the health aspects in sickness. Under the current medical model, many deviations from the norm become deviants. From a process oriented paradigm the extraordinary complexities of a life with its turns and twists, its failings and diseases, are valued for their contribution to diversity and for the learning the assortment of puzzle pieces provides to the whole. I want to validate the immense benefits and successes of modern medicine and enhance our thinking in psychology and medicine seeking to further our understanding of Process and diversity.

Imagine a doctor or therapist who says: drink this tea, take this medicine or supplement, let's do this surgery, *and* let's find out what that pounding, spasm, irritation, discoloring is all about. Let's find out what your symptoms are teaching us. Can you make a gesture that expresses how your pain feels? Tell me your story, and let's see how your symptom fits into the wholeness of your life. Let's get rid of this nasty itch *and* let's play a game in which you can be as irritating as you want. Tell me what you dreamed last night and let's figure out how your dream figures relate to your illness. Who in your family, co-workers and friends annoys you in the same way your symptom energy bugs you? Let's think together what your symptom wants you to do in the world. I want you to do more physical exercise and understand what is good to not exercise in your life. I recommend you lose some weight and put more weight into that relationship or work situation.

There is health-in-sickness; it's not only pathology. Today's main medical paradigm that sees disease as a result of genetics and environment omits something essential—the particularity of our Process. We are not just the result of hereditary and societal forces, and our medical biography is not only determined by the plot written by our genetic code, ancestral heredity, trauma and social circumstances. We all bear uniqueness and a gift, something essential that asks to be lived. Paradoxically, illness and disease can be a wakeup call to live our gift to the world. Individuality and diversity are the defining images and characters that the world needs to learn as a whole organism. Without them, there would be no awareness and growth. Our uniqueness (including all our faults, failures and illnesses) is in part what allows us to learn from each other and to grow as a community. Each of us is a unique puzzle piece with a slightly different shape, color and pattern.

Together, we form the puzzle. I learn from you and you learn from me. My illness is a gift for myself that allows me to learn about my inner diversity, such as my tree bark nature that compensates for my softer and gentler side. It is also a gift for my environment that allows us to learn together about helping each other and setting boundaries (see my toe nail example in the introduction). Our pathologies are as authentic as the healthy rest of us; they are part of our gift, image or character. Hence, this book is about processes that contain health and sickness. It is about offering a way to regard both health and sickness differently, to enter their story and information and to discover in their pain and beauty what they might be indicating.

Health-in-sickness and sickness-in health applies to individuals as well as communities. As we learn to appreciate our particular gifts, we also learn from the characters we encounter on our journey. Many people act like symptoms and enrich our path through life by challenging us to embrace more diversity. In *The Dignity of Difference* Jonathan Sacks (2002) emphasizes the world's need for ecological and human diversity. There is an evolutionary need for biodiversity. I claim that there is an evolutionary need for human and knowledge diversity. Teilhard de Chardin said that evolution won't be driven by physical adaptation but by human consciousness, creativity and spirit. Part of that development is propelled by conflicts and struggles with human diversity. Social disparities cause human suffering and poor health. They also offer occasions for community involvement and development.

I advocate for a health model that includes disease, sickness and injury as part of health and being fit and healthy. Disorder and disturbances are ubiquitous and continuously challenge the steady state or homeostatic state of health. We are healthy only despite all the health challenges or only when we embrace the constant state of disorder we are in. Any athlete knows that injury is part of his or her future. Diseases and injuries are unavoidable and part of everybody's experience. Preventing disease or injuries is not entirely possible. Thus, the question is not only how can we prevent or avoid diseases and injuries but how can we integrate sickness and injuries in our experience of health and fitness?

Health is a norm and vision. As such, it creates a direction and motivational pull for us to overcome our health challenges and injuries. Without this vision there is no reason for change and improvement.

Health is an aspect of our life force and drive that motivates us to get up in the morning and exercise; avoid coffee, alcohol and nicotine; and eat our greens. As a cultural norm, it is also coercive and marginalizes many other experiences that also come with life. Health as the norm shames and bullies those who are less privileged health-wise. Some of us—and all of us at some point—are less fortunate and succumb to sickness and injury. Health as an ideal state negates all other reality and lived experience.

In our culture, symptoms mean something "bad." But the word itself means accidental happening, neither good nor bad. As accidental happenings, symptoms belong in the realm of destiny and not medicine alone. Our relationship to them need not be a moral one but also one of curiosity and interest about their expression of diversity.

If a symptom is not only bad, we can open ourselves up to its image or information. This allows us to open our eyes to the intention in a symptom. If symptoms lose their moral connotation as wrong, we can approach them with less anxiety and simply as a phenomenon or experience. A friend of mine shared his experience with a knee injury. He is an avid runner and while running strained his knee. He experienced his injured knee as stiff and unbending. My friend's inner majority favors flexibility. His inner norm is supported by an outer cultural majority that also tends to prefer flexibility over rigidity. His own inner diversity struggle mirrors a cultural and political process.

Another friend shared her problem with blurred vision. When she took off her glasses and amplified the blurriness, she experienced a kind of "hallucination." In that experience, she also developed a great relationship with the group that she was part of. Her primary identity was one of being shy and sensitive to other's feedback. Without her glasses, she became less sensitive to feedback and was able to discover her more visionary and psychic nature. Many people develop vision problems with age. We can interpret these as a natural deterioration of the eyes' elasticity, or we can take these vision problems to mean that as we age we may want to focus less on details but rather direct our attention to the bigger picture.

Our symptoms and illnesses, the burnout we feel when we are overworked or overwhelmed, the moods and anxieties we experience in relationships: these are all disturbances and troubles that need to be put right, and they are vulnerabilities that can help us transform the way we live and relate. Without challenges and vulnerabilities we remain in the dark. There is health-in-sickness and as we will see, sickness-in-health.

## Sickness-in-Health

Concepts of health and how we as a culture define health influence our body experience individually and collectively. What we consider to be health is culturally defined and a highly political issue. On the other hand, our bodies are deeply democratic and value diversity. Through the experiences that they convey they show us alternate realities. Again, mainstream ideas about health and the cultural concepts of good health are by themselves stressors and add stress and daily hassles to the lives of people facing illness and disability. If, in our beliefs about health, we exclude the symptom experience we help co-create and solidify the disease experiences in others.

Thinking about health as something that one-sidedly needs to be safeguarded and restored distracts us from the diversity experience embedded in the illness or symptom experience. By merely thinking that something is wrong we are part of the problem for ourselves and others. Recently, I have worked with a couple of people who suffer from an attention deficit and hyperactivity problem. They suffer because they are made to believe there is something wrong with them, they are not normal and their behaviors are troublesome. They grew up with the expectation that they could think linearly and perform tasks one step at a time. But their brains worked differently. Their brains could think multiple thoughts at the same time and jump from one subject to another. Their families, doctors, teachers and the whole culture around them didn't understand or support their process and made them feel sick and abnormal to the point that they became sick or adopted the identity of being sick. David Finch in his *Journal of Best Practices* (2012) describes very eloquently how he struggles to muster his life with Asperger's Syndrome and how he and his wife cope with the multitude of peculiarities that come with Asperger's. Finch differentiates between the world of neurotypicals and his experience in what he calls Aspergerland.

Asperger's and ADHD are their own cultures, ethnic groups or tribes. They come with a diversity experience and are not mere illnesses. Problems occur because we "neurotypicals," or the mainstream of the population, define a world that is normal within the borders of mainstream land and normality. A society that both sets the standards and expects everybody to meet them separates the culture of the accepted normal and healthy from the culture of the sick. But if we recognize and value the behavioral and perceptual differences that people with autism and ADHD express, we have to question the definition of "normal." People in Aspergerland or ADHDland have a different experience with brains that process information and function differently. Individuals with ADHD strive in high-stress environments such as crises or emergency rooms. They are very good at solving multiple problems and jumping from one task to the other. They are not sick or abnormal but different. People with Asperger's and ADHD ultimately help us broaden the concept of what it means to be human.

The illness geography includes an asthmaland, ulcerland, cancerland, etc. The world not only comprises weight typicals, body shape typicals, blood sugar typicals, blood pressure typicals, health typicals or normotypicals. The disease of the normotypicals is to think there is such a normality world; in reinforcing the beliefs about normality, normotypicals help co-create illness and suffering in others.

Health differences do not require us to sacrifice connectedness. As we confront our own beliefs about what is typically healthy or normal, what is abnormal or unnatural and what values inform our beliefs, we can and do still belong to each other. Many individuals with health challenges embrace their diagnosis as a vibrant and worthy aspect of their being that extends beyond their feeling victimized by an impairment. Asperger's, ADHD and other neurodiverse or healthdiverse conditions are an identity the world should welcome and adapt to. They are also diagnoses that entail suffering, impairment and loss. For one person they are an affliction and for another they are his or her identity. I believe in the deep worth of the illness experience and the diversity it expresses and teaches us. We would impoverish the world if we were to eliminate these culturally specific and diverse experiences. Many sick and differently abled people are content in who they are and how they think. We have an obligation to respond to those people's self-esteem with respect. By claiming the land of normality, so-called healthy people push the neurodiverse and healthdiverse into the margins of society.

Mainstream beliefs about body shape, body image, attractivity and sexuality produce shame and self-hatred in people who don't conform to the expectations and standards. This has important health implications. I am currently counseling a woman who has internalized all these beliefs. She describes herself as being short, overweight and unattractive. She is depressed and lonely and feels stuck in a self-destructive binge-eating pattern. She has many stories of being shamed for how she looks. She wants to eat less and lose weight but is afraid of how her upper arms, belly and breasts will look once she has lost weight. She knows how her skin will sag in various parts of her body and how people will react to her looks. She is afraid that once she is skinnier men might approach her and then be disappointed with her looks. She would rather stay overweight and prevent the shameful experience.

She feels stuck in a depressed state and is seeking comfort and soothing from her despair by engaging in addictive behaviors such as computer gaming and overeating. She describes her physical experience of depression as a neck and back tension that pushes her down with an inner voice stating:"Hold on, stay safe, the world outside is violent." She wishes for some *joie de vivre* which she imagines gaining through social connection and engagement in the world. But the world is too scary and unsafe, and she avoids it for fear of being abused again. She remembers an overweight dog trainer she saw in a show who moved with pride. Relating to her, she can connect with her own anger and passion to fight back the internalized oppressive thoughts and beliefs about her weight. Her individual process brings her back to her inalienable power, the life force that keeps her getting up in the morning despite her despair.

Recently, she shared how one time she was in a group of people after a lecture and was drawn to talk to a man she liked, someone who was as short as herself and seemed interesting. Then a conventionally attractive young man started to talk to her, which she found flattering. She felt compelled to keep talking to the younger man and noticed how the other man gave up and turned away. She was overcome by the perceived "compliment," one she knew was motivated by the cultural values she usually rejected herself because of how they generally made her feel.

Shame is the opposite of empathy and self-love. Shame says: "I am bad, wrong, not good enough, too skinny, too heavy, too short, etc."

Empathy or compassion says: "I am enough, I am worthy of love, belonging and joy; I am worthy now, not if, not when, right this minute, as is." We are all vulnerable to other people's criticism and judgments. We react by being defensive, protecting ourselves behind accomplishments, degrees, titles and by pushing ourselves to be perfect. Body shame and our privilege to offset societal judgments are closely linked to the amount of sexual, physical and emotional abuse we experienced in our past. If parents or loved ones carried out the abuse, self-defeating feelings and behaviors can be an unconscious way to side with the perpetrator in an attempt to gain their love by saying: "See, I agree with you. Can you now love me?" Examining and confronting the abuse is then a prerequisite to developing self-love and compassion.

Embracing our imperfections and "failings" and allowing ourselves to disappoint and be vulnerable is made harder by cultural and social standards and beliefs. Individual work has to be complemented with community work. Open forums and group processes are a good way to address these important issues on a community level. We all share the tension between cultural expectations and our inner path.

### *Archetype of the Invalid*

Guggenbühl-Craig (1999) speaks of a basic process of life that resists all healing efforts. He calls it the "archetype of the invalid." Failings, functional impairments and symptoms are always part of us. He regards health and invalidity as complementary archetypal fantasies and criticizes the fact that wholeness has been identified one-sidedly with health. He argues that the prevailing idea that health is wholeness in mind and body ignores the processes of disease and invalidity that are within each of us. Separating health from illness leads to a one-sided focus on health and wholeness and to negative stereotyping of people with symptoms. As neurotypical, normotypical or healthy people we think we have neurological and other developments and states that are consistent with what most people would perceive as normal. Our implicit assumption of this being the norm and that our experience of the world is either the only one or the only correct one reinforces the marginalization of people with less health privileges. Our lack of awareness allows for the body to become a symbolic field for the reproduction of mainstream values and conceptions about health and normality.

In Guggenbühl-Craig's opinion, the body may also be a site for resistance to, and transformation of, those systems of meanings. Sickness may be an unconscious expression of a struggle to resist and defend ourselves from the one-sided moralistic call for good total health. The ambition to heal everyone and everything forces a counteraction that resists the expectations of wholeness and good health.

The one-sided centrality of "good" health discriminates against ill and disabled people and those whose inner states and experiences are less strong and resilient. It also contributes to the isolation of individuals and families who experience health challenges, disability and unusual states of consciousness. The focus on health and healing and the emphasis on recovery to normal deny the validity of the lived illness or "disability." Narrow values of health and normality and unrealistic medical ambitions to restore health no matter what oppress everybody—the sick *and* the healthy. Disease and illness, as well as people afflicted by disease and illness, are teachers of our common humanness and diversity. Someone with ADHD or Asperger's or any other illness has a teaching. My friend's unbending knee teaches me about boundaries; my other friend's vision problem makes it easier for me to trust altered states of consciousness. In his book *Living on the Edge,* Joe Goodbread (2009) describes in detail the medical process of diagnosing and its psychological and social implications. Illness provokes anxiety, and the less certain and explicable an illness is the more we feel out of control and at the mercy of random events. Giving a context, name, rationale and significance to a process, which may otherwise feel frightening and out of control, allows us to regain a measure of power and control. This is why many people feel relieved when they receive a diagnosis, even when that diagnosis is dreadful and the prognosis bad. A diagnosis is often an explanation, and we hope that it also will lead to a treatment and remedy.

On the other hand, a diagnosis changes the dynamic process of a body experience into a fixed state. By substituting a name or state for what is experienced as a fluid process, a diagnosis can limit the possible outcomes. Attached to the diagnosis are explanations of the origin and causes of a body experience and ideas about treatment options and their prognosis. These are implicit beliefs that create expectations, act as placebo or nocebo and influence outcomes. Medical diagnoses are the consensus reality classifications of body experiences. They instill specific meanings to subjective body experiences that are fluid. These meanings are helpful, complicate and at times limiting.

Diagnoses also separate you from me. They make you have a problem and be sick while I can remain under the illusion of being healthy or normal. They create a boundary between you and me and delegate you into illnessland with its new "ethnicity." In contrast, *Ubuntu* and *deep democracy*[54] recognize our interdependence and the fact that our humanity is intertwined with the humanity of others. Our separation is artificial and illusionary. If I am human because I live through you and you are in Aspergerland, I must be somehow there, too. If I share your humanity, I have more difficulty in maintaining the border between normalland and Aspergerland.

Illness and disease can be powerful connectors and make us all more humane. They force us to relate to our feelings and emotions and open us to aspects of life that aren't completely controllable and solvable.

A narrow social justice perspective that sees health disparities and oversees the implicit strengths of marginalized and underprivileged communities is also a problem: it patronizes and disempowers the very people we want to help. It solidifies the experience of marginality. Social problems and public health symptoms are also a community dreaming process of diversity. In the disparity, there is something wrong that needs rectification, *and* there is something right or meaningful that needs awareness and help with processing.

Public health issues need advocacy and support to move a step further, one that goes beyond health equity. Open forums and group processes are a great way to expand the individual and health advocacy work. Ubuntu is a great framework for weaving individual work into community work. Our individual processes and struggles with health and illness are relevant for everybody. Because there is so much shame and abuse around the body, bringing our vulnerabilities and struggles out of the closet into a friendly public forum can be healing in itself. Our health problems are teachers for the community. "It's all one tea, but the experience of the tea is different" (Schupbach 2012, personal communication). Working on our own "cup of tea" in a group context can be an illuminating experience for everybody. Concepts of parallel worlds and Ubuntu are useful for crossing the borders between cultural illness experiences, going from the individual to the community

54 See chapter V.

and learning from each other. Individual and group work enhance each other.

As patients, we project medical solutions as outside of our sphere of influence and outside of ourselves. They become third parties that are split from our individual consciousness. Medical treatments, procedures and cures are by themselves also dreaming processes that we share with our providers. As patients, we can profit from taking the projections back and integrating them into our own healing process, belief system and culture. A colleague of mine shared that she had dreamed a co-worker was having a medical crisis two nights before this co-worker had a seizure at the office. Our bodies and minds are non-locally intertwined and we are all part of a common ground or environing world. Medical procedures and systems are part of that shared dreaming field.

## *Health-Care or Sick-Care?*

Most current medical systems are sick-care systems—they treat the sick and cure the symptoms. They are not health-care systems that foster health and prevent sickness and injuries. Many existing sick-care systems reimburse providers based on the individual activities, interventions and services. The more you do or perform the more you get paid. They incentivize quantity over quality. Health care reform movements in Europe and the US attempt to shift from a sick-care to a health-care system and to move from reimbursing quantity to valuing quality. Global budgets are replacing actuarially sound capitated rates, which allow for more prevention and flexible care plans that could, for example, pay for an air conditioner to prevent heart failure and expensive emergency room visits. They also could pay for an emergency room lawyer who can help families write letters to their landlords asking for mold sanitation to prevent their children's asthma attacks. The new focus is on paying for value and performance instead of individual services. Providers are held accountable for the outcomes and health value they can produce. Ideally, communities and providers come together to define what health outcomes they want to achieve and how they want to get there.

Such structural health reform efforts in Denmark led to the consolidation of 14 counties into 5 regions, 272 into 98 municipalities and the closing of more than 70 hospitals and a substantial reduction of available hospital beds. You can imagine this goes against many particular interests and triggers a lot of resistance from individuals and institutions who have a lot to lose. Similar efforts are happening here in Oregon, where I live. Discussions have started about the goals the communities would like to achieve and the care plans needed to accomplish these outcomes. The efforts are inspired by a need to reduce budgetary deficits and limit the increase in health care costs. The vision is to accomplish a triple aim of reducing costs, improving care and giving people more access to health services. This effort is led by a group of highly motivated individuals and headed by our governor, who is a physician. But, so far, health care recipients have rarely been included in the discussion. The reforms are perceived as mandated by state and federal governments, which provokes a lot of resistance to what is perceived as generating more government involvement and limiting individual choice.

For providers, the health care reform requires them to change their culture of providing services. In the past, they were in the comfortable position of define what were needed and paid-for services. Now, they must become more accountable, justify the need for services and their medical necessity and link them to outcome targets. The buzz words are treat to target, pay for performance and evidence-based practice. Because of budgetary limits, services need to be efficient and effective.

But the processes that help restore and maintain health follow nonlinear multi-causal paths and are embedded in a complex system of social, environmental, behavioral and genetic factors. It is easy to delineate wished-for outcomes but very difficult to draw the path to achieve these outcomes. Reducing the obesity incidence of a population, for example, is clearly a goal that would improve health. As we all know, this goal is very difficult to accomplish on an individual level and even harder on a population level. Behaviorists are now focusing on health or wellness coaching and have come up with multiple good strategies to lose weight. They often work but are very hard to sustain over time. Most people will regain lost weight in very little time. Body weight is linked to social, community and economic factors; ethnic identity, body image, gender roles, emotional states, addictions and more. To increase success rates, individualized behavioral approaches need to be complemented with community-based ones that involve the community in making choices.

Commonly, system or policy reforms happen through advocacy. Individual groups identify issues that need change and recruit support for the new ideas and policies. Parties fight for their particular interests and constituencies. Many would agree that our health care system is sick; it is too costly and inequitable. If we look at it from a different angle, it is not sick and bad but injured. From that perspective, a new Process viewpoint emerges that doesn't ask what's wrong but instead what happened. In addition to focusing on the cure, the new paradigm asks about the story, the physical, emotional, social and moral injuries and how they happened. It involves the protagonists to create a narrative and recruits them to engage in a process of recovery. Community participation is the core of this process of identifying the injuries and delineating the path toward recovery. Community dialogues and open forums are the vessels for this participatory project. Both emphasize the importance of creating a safe space for mutual sharing of experiences, stories and knowledge and the need for openness to listening to all sides and viewpoints. This sharing has to incorporate the feelings of participants, as injuries always come with some pain and suffering and healing occurs in shared pain and suffering. In community dialogues, we are all co-learners in a mutual process of participation and learning from each other; we build community and collaboration. Practical problem-solving strategies are then grounded in a mutual understanding of each other.

In 2011 and 2012, I facilitated three African refugee community and health care provider dialogues. Participants included 125 representatives from eight African countries (Burundi, Ethiopia, Ghana, Kenya, Nigeria, Rwanda, Senegal and Somalia), as well as medical providers from various local clinics, public health departments, medical schools and community-based social work agencies. The invitation described the goals of learning about each other's cultures, values and beliefs.

In the dialogues, African participants expressed to the providers the need for establishing trust and raised many concerns about inadequate access to translation services and inappropriate interpretation facilitators. Men and women discussed the importance of culturally specific norms about appropriate gender roles, culturally acceptable behaviors and expectations and men's health. Participants also discussed the lack of understanding of preventive health care, stressed the different needs of refugees and immigrants and raised awareness about problems with self-advocacy and empowerment and the need for policy advocacy. African community members also expressed their need to personalize connections with health providers in the first few moments of a meeting in order to build a level of comfort and a trusting environment. Participants also expressed the need for healing touch, eye contact and thoughtful greeting.

Providers expressed frustrations with some of their cultural and language limitations and shared stories of leaving work knowing they hadn't done justice to the newly arriving refugees in their care. At the end, everybody gave us feedback of renewed hope and motivation to embark on a process of recovery.

In mainstream open forums, people are invited to share their viewpoints and stories. They often lack a culture of facilitated interaction and dialogue. People feel safe to express themselves knowing that they will be heard out and not interrupted. Process oriented open forums and group processes add a culture of facilitated interaction and dialogue between the different voices. They invite people to share their experiences and feelings and engage in a dialogue, which can become emotional and requires trained facilitators who are able to keep the group safe while participants are examining some of the roots of their conflicts. Through dialogue and the processing of feelings, a new sense of community can emerge and often participants will develop leadership and propose corrective actions.

A community health-in sickness or sickness-in-health model welcomes the relationship between polarized views. It incorporates a deeper understanding based on a "whole stage" concept. The whole stage is needed to understand and create the communal play. It invites difference and diverging positions as a means to a greater understanding of the diversity of nature, which we need to evolve and develop as a group, organization, community and world.

Health and health care are commons[55]—finite, common property resources that are shared by all. Viewing health care as a commons means that we all have to change our perceptions, beliefs, and behav-

---

55 Commons refers to the cultural and natural resources accessible to all members of a community, including natural materials such as air, water and a habitable earth. These resources are held in common, not owned privately.

iors in regard to health and health care. If one imagines health care delivery and the money required to maintain a system that provides care equally to everyone, as a commons—that is, a public system with finite resources—we all have to take responsibility for the well-being of the commons. We all must think about how resources are used in an overall sense, for if we don't there won't be enough health care dollars for everyone. So while concentrating on what we as individuals need, we also have to think on the commons level about the benefit and well-being of the community at large.

From a "commons" or community perspective, many health care systems struggle with individuals who drain care and money from the public system. In the US, many uninsured use hospital emergency rooms to receive care[56]. The cost of this care eventually gets passed on to those who do have health insurance, either in the form of higher premiums or denial of coverage by an insurance company. Another issue is that individually, physicians, patients and families are unable to set limits on the utilization of medical resources. When you are sick it is difficult to think about how your personal utilization of care affects others. That is why communities are now establishing global budgets for health care and guidelines for the utilization of care. One can say that treating health and heath care as a commodity is immoral, but everybody will behave "egotistically" when sick. The community responsibility or commons perspective struggles with the individual perspective that seeks the best care possible. Communities need to come together to process these roles in the field and find individual community solutions to distribute care within limited budgets. A scary and often marginalized role is the one who maximizes profit and takes advantage of the weakness or sickness of others. The tension lies between the polarized viewpoints of profit versus public good. From a process oriented understanding, we share the role of the profiteer and the one that gives back to the collective. From an expanded commons perspective, we examine all the shared roles in a specific context or field and let them interact with each other to examine their deeper meaning. The fact that these roles are still so polarized means that we as communities haven't yet resolved the existing conflicts and haven't found a balance between community responsibility and individual needs.

---

56 In the US, a hospital is obligated to treat anyone who comes to its emergency room.

A community or commons attitude leads to rationing care and focusing on health problems that are frequent and whose treatments will return the biggest public health value for the investment. This attitude marginalizes the individual who faces a rare and costly health problem. I remember a few years ago the situation of a very sick young person who needed a combined heart and lung transplant. Her public insurance, which had adopted a selective list of covered procedures, was willing to pay for both interventions separately but not when done in one combined surgery. This led to a huge public outcry in the press, which forced the insurance company to rethink its policies. That was a typical example of a conflict between the public versus the individual good. How can a community "sacrifice" the welfare of one of its members for the sake of the benefit of the group? Paradoxically, these kinds of decisions happen silently all the time but once they become public they are difficult to sustain. Another example is the marginalization of rare and orphan diseases[57]. By definition, in the United States, a rare and orphan disease is one that affects fewer than 200,000 individuals at any given time. Because of the small population afflicted the illness, funding to investigate causes and treatments is limited, which slows the discovery of potential therapies. Yet there are over 7,000 recognized rare diseases and an estimated 350 million people worldwide who are affected by them at any given time. This again shows that health inequities are complex, broad and difficult to rectify. We need more places to discuss them publicly and to develop community-based solutions.

What does a non-pathological and deeply democratic health care system look like? Well, this is a new model and no one person can propose such a model because it must be developed by the communities themselves. By asking the question, I indirectly make a one-sided and polarized statement. This is a group process and will need community participation. One existing change model is based on Noriaki Kano's model (1984) of improvement and aims at: 1) reducing defects and identifying what doesn't work (i.e., the widespread problem of central line infections); 2) reducing costs while maintaining experience; and 3) developing new products, strategies and services. Based on that model some propose possible ways of improvement in health care.

57 Rare or orphan diseases affect not enough people or the people affected live in underdeveloped countries, so that the developments of cures is financially not viable for drug companies.

They include reducing overtreatment (i.e., too many x-rays, antibiotics for viral infections, etc.), addressing the barriers to coordinating care and failings in care delivery, reducing excessive administrative costs and health care processes and fighting fraud and abuse. Anticipated threats to the change model are imagined "defectors" or non-compliant partners, a fear of the public perception such as an antipathy toward evidence-based medical practices, neglect of safety net services for the marginalized poor and resistance to change from special interest groups such as hospitals and providers with specialized services.

These are great ideas that deserve our support and efforts to help generate the necessary changes. In addition, if you look at this strategy and analysis from a process oriented and system-theory perspective, it is clear that all the identified problems and suggested strategies are actually complex group processes.

The issue of overtreatment and defensive medicine is based on the fear of litigation and malpractice suits, and we all participate in that process. Many political efforts to reduce litigation and cap the awarded amount of damages, so called tort[58] reforms, have failed because proponents want to keep granting victims of medical errors enough compensation and believe that a fear of lawsuits acts as deterrence and prevents errors. They see the benefit of defensive medicine, which is rooted in the goal of avoiding mistakes. But, besides contributing to increasing costs, each additional procedure or test, no matter how cautiously performed, opens a new possibility of error. X-rays, CT and MRI scans can lead to false positives and unnecessary operations, with additional risk of complications like infections and bleeding. Each new prescribed medication comes with added side effects, interactions and the danger of allergic reactions.

In medicine, such as in other professions, negligence and mistakes lead to damages. But in medicine, these damages always directly affect someone's physical integrity, which is laden with emotions. We all make mistakes, sometimes unintentionally, sometimes negligently, sometimes recklessly, and our mistakes have consequences. The amount of risk and possible opportunities for mistakes make the prac-

---

58 Tort actions are civil common law claims first created in the English commonwealth system as a non-legislative means for compensating wrongs and harm done by one party to another's person, property or other protected interest.

tice of medicine stressful. Providers often internalize the pressure and defensiveness and keep second guessing themselves, which on one hand is good and on the other hand bad because nobody works well under too much pressure. How to develop trust in oneself and project trust for patients in an environment or field that is fraught with uncertainty is a complex relationship process. Trust is based on relationships, and this is perhaps the one area patients, providers and the public marginalize most. We all share the onus of that relationship and by leaving the "malpractice" issue in the hands of doctors and lawyers and by neglecting the relationships with our doctors, we all participate in the problem.

The defectors and non-compliant partners are roles in the medical force field with valid concerns and points of view. The public is likely to rightfully sense the limitations of evidence-based medicine and to ask for a deepening of the discussion of evidence and what it means. The issue of a safety net for the uninsured and poor is long-standing and has been debated for years. Some see a necessity to strengthen individual responsibility and accountability and others value the collective responsibility to care for the poor. All these issues are large collective debates and processes that require cultural consensus building. Conventional democratic processes have so far failed to help resolve these issues as they elicit resistance in the side that has been outnumbered.

A typical organizational development statement says: "Improvement is change but not all change is improvement; if you don't like the result change the system." The essence of this statement is that change is a process and needs to take feedback into account. In the current health care debates and reform propositions, progressive transformers (the new health care innovators) are compared with conservative preservatives, incumbent health care players that want to keep the status quo. From a pathological framework, the preservatives are perceived as outmoded and hanging onto privileges and particular interests. While this may be true for some, the conservative viewpoint may also represent a valuable perspective that could inform and improve the reformists' agenda. Systems comprise roles that are created by the field (i.e., the larger unconscious wholeness) that brings about these perspectives and viewpoints to develop awareness and learn about itself. Besides changing the non-working systems and advocating for the changes we want, it can be helpful if we at times change our attitudes toward each other and learn to see ourselves in the other. Some people do bad things, are abusive, take advantage of others and the environment and have bad ideas that need to be improved. And, we are all collectively responsible for our health care, our communities, the environment, and the world.

Our health systems are in a transition from volume to value (reimbursing value-based outcomes instead of the volume of interventions), from sick care to health care, from disease-centric to patient- and population-centric. Today, the 5 percent of frail elderly, the poly-chronic ill people and the often uninsured urban poor account for 45 percent of health care expenditures. Much of the efforts to contain health care costs are now focusing on the so called "hot spots" of high utilization of health care dollars. Expanding insurance coverage; coordinating care through medical home[59] models; addressing root causes such as poverty, homelessness, access to nutritious food and exercise opportunities; reducing systemic disparities based on racism and homophobia; and so on are the multiple approaches that are required to make a difference. Health care reforms are closely tied to social justice and health equity issues. A population-centric approach will require a new form of community involvement and participation to tackle these community relationship issues. The deep democracy concepts outlined in chapter IV can be valuable tools to help find true community-based solutions.

## *Positive Deviance*

Positive Deviance, an approach to social change based on individuals and programs that are uncommonly successful and were able to develop better solutions than their peers, is another tool for individual and community change. Starbucks collaborated with Virginia Mason Hospital and Medical Center in Seattle to reduce costs and improve value of care. To improve the treatment of chronic back pain in Starbucks employees, they focused on physical therapy. That new approach led to new processes, including same-day visits (as opposed to 31-day waits),

59 The medical home, also known as the patient-centered medical home (PCMH), is an integrated multi-disciplinary health care delivery model led by a physician, physician assistant or nurse practitioner that provides comprehensive and continuous medical care to patients with the goal of obtaining improved health outcomes.

reduced use of imaging tests and prescription drugs and the addition of psychological support. Within three months, 94 percent of Starbucks employees with back-pain complaints were back at work within a day.

Other care groups have developed new models of delivering care. One group in California (CareMore) prevents falls by providing elderly patients with regular podiatric care (i.e., toenail clipping) and by removing dangerous rugs. Patients are given iPhones that allow them to participate in conference calls with healthcare professionals and are remotely monitored with devices that feed data automatically to doctors. For example, patients with congestive heart failure are given a wireless scale that reports their weight on a daily basis[60]. They have singing pillboxes that chime when it's time to take medications.

> These unusual tactics produce enviable outcomes: CareMore's hospitalization rate is 24 percent below average, hospital stays are 38 percent shorter than average, and the amputation rate among diabetics is 60 percent below average. Overall member costs are roughly 18 percent below the Medicare average. (Main and Slywotsky 2012, 2)

Their research asserts that this type of patient-centered medicine, which focuses on coordinated care, highest-cost cases and upstream prevention, can improve outcomes by 20 to 60 percent and cut costs by 15 to 30 percent.

Positive Deviance is something we all can utilize individually and collectively. We all know of an individual or group that was able to handle a problem or situation with unusual success. Some of us have had this experience ourselves. We can learn from our peers and from our own past "peer" behavior. Imagine adopting a solution or behavior and consider the barriers that stand in the way. Do that as individuals, groups, teams and communities with your own health problems. Don't wait; be creative and courageous, and dare greatly.

What is best for the patient? What is best for the community? What is best for the environment? What is best for the world? Can anybody think that holistically? Probably not as individuals, but perhaps as a community we can.

---

60 Weight gain is a key sign of congestive heart failure, and early recognition is a key step to preventing hospitalization.

8

# *Conclusion*

*As a tree torn from the soil, as a river separated from its source, the human soul wanes when detached from what is greater than itself.*

Abraham Joshua Heschel (1954, 6)

*It is in the process of embracing our imperfections that we find our truest gifts: courage, compassion and connection.*

Brené Brown (2010, 58)

*Ring the bells that still can ring*
*Forget your perfect offering*
*There is a crack in everything*
*That's how the light gets in.*

Leonard Cohen, "Anthem"

*The wound is the place where the Light enters you.*

Rumi

*I try to be smart, but feel best when clouded. I am an altered wanderer, because I follow something no one sees. Like you, I seek stability, but in my depths, I flow with the waves. Why? Because after resisting, it's easier to follow that invisible choreographer and her zigzag stirrings of that endless breeze.*

Arnold Mindell, class notes from Processwork and the Mystery of Tao, February 2013

In general, we don't *feel* health. Being healthy, we take health for granted and, unaware of its presence, we believe it to be a natural state. We are reminded of its value when we lose health and get sick. As such, illness always comes with a loss. Now, could there be a gain in illness or health in sickness as the title of this book suggests? Nobody wants to be voluntarily sick. Illness is too unpleasant, annoying and painful and disturbs our normal course of life. That is why we all strive to prevent its occurrence and minimize the resulting pain and suffering.

The goal of medicine is to preserve health and recover health from sickness. To determine the extent of its field and boundaries of work, medicine has to define what it means by health. And because medicine is a cultural phenomenon in which we all participate, we as a community need to come up with our own definitions. The World Health Organization (WHO 1946) defines health: "… (as) a state of complete physical, mental, and social well-being and not merely the absence of disease or infirmity." Complete physical, mental and social well-being is a powerful vision, and it is utterly too big of a scope for helping medicine achieve its goal of health. The social determinants of health are extremely important and they go way beyond what medicine can tackle on its own. Medicine has a role in addressing them and needs to join forces with other social and cultural systems and the collective at large to move toward the ideal of complete social well-being.

As humans we have the innate ability to be self-aware, to have subjective experiences and differentiate ourselves from the external world of objects. This awareness also allows us to experience our limitations and to become conscious of our mortality. This experience of ultimate boundaries is threatening and shocking and illnesses are constant reminders of this anxiety-provoking ultimate fate we can't avoid. But the boundaries of death and sickness are also challenges that wake us up to find meaning. Without them, we would lose ourselves in the oblivion of well-being.

Nietzsche fought against sickness all his life, and this process shaped his philosophy and understanding of health. He differentiated between a small health of physical and mental well-being and a *big health* that contained sickness. He saw sickness ultimately as an opportunity for a deepening of self-awareness and a change in attitude toward life. Life, he said, needs sickness as a fishhook for awareness. Because of illness we lose trust in life, which then becomes a motivating energy that paradoxically allows us to participate in and rediscover life despite illness.

Boundaries, problems, failings, imperfections and illnesses are stimulants of life; they are our teachers, or what Carlos Castaneda called petty tyrants. We need them to wake up, and by overcoming and integrating them we deepen our lives. Sickness is a component of health and we are only in good health if we can allow ourselves to be sick and learn from it. As such we are an ill healthy person.

We can now return to the WHO definition of health and understand it as addressing a utopian ideal of being comprehensively healed, which mirrors the ideal of Nietzsche's big health. Piet van Spijk (2011) defines health as one's ability to lead a meaningful life. Health-in-sickness and sickness-in-health is an attempt to propose ways to use our boundaries, problems, failings, imperfections and illnesses to achieve big health, or meaning. A medicine that embraces Process and our existential limitations will learn to examine its own boundaries and the confines that come with diversity and relationship issues. Medical providers will strengthen their skills of small medicine and develop the awareness of a new meaning dimension in big medicine. Medical systems will reconsider their organizational, social and cultural frontiers and develop new participatory relationships with communities and other systems to approach the collective issues of big health. In addition to advancing their recovery technology, the new systems will cultivate new relationship awareness and cultural competency, and respect the dignity of difference. Big medicine will also confront the margins of its responsibility, as it will never be able to restore a meaningful life to everybody. It remains our own individual responsibility to take charge of our process and empower ourselves to lead a meaningful life. Big medicine can only provide a helping hand for that. We all share the onus to take care of the consensus reality aspects of small medicine and small health, to step into the parallel world of big medicine and big health. Let's begin the journey of discovering meaning by being curious about our own and our communities' Processes.

Rabbi Heschel (1961) remarked in a speech:

> What a person lives by is not only a sense of belonging but also a sense of indebtedness. The need to be needed corresponds to a fact: something is asked of every person. Advancing in years must not be taken to mean a process of suspending the requirements and commitments under which a person lives.

We all have a calling, something the world is asking us to be or do. To be needed, to feel connected and to participate in our communities is meaningful; it protects our health and doesn't stop with age or illness. My calling is to share my thoughts about a new health and medical model and attitude that are based on Process and community. Health and illness are processes that extend beyond the consensually accepted real world of objects and parts, of normality and abnormality, of individuals and communities. Disease and illness are real; they hurt and threaten. We need to take them seriously, protect ourselves and our communities, prevent them the best we can and get help to treat them and recover. Only then can we, with kindness and compassion, examine their meaning for us individually and as a community. From a Process perspective, disease and illness are mysterious; they bring forth aspects of our diversity. They are cracks, imperfections that let the light in and can bring us the gifts of courage, compassion and connection. They can bring us closer to our common humanity and answer our soul's call for connecting to something greater than ourselves. I don't want to minimize the pain and suffering that comes with illness, and I want us all to be smart and do our best to recover and stay healthy. Only after doing our best can we let go and follow the flow of experience and its wisdom. Push hard, work hard and when tired, hopeless, depressed and burned out, forget your perfect offering and remember the wonder of that endless breeze that carries you in her mysterious ways.

In *The Dignity of Difference,* Jonathan Sacks says "if we were completely different there could be no communication but if we were totally the same we would have nothing to say" (2002, 18).

If we were always healthy, if there was no diversity, there would be no motivation to learn and develop. We need more dialogue to understand our diversity. We need to develop skills to listen to our bodies' stories. We need forums where we can engage in respectful and reciprocal conversations to learn about our community issues. But dialogue may not be enough since dialogue can't always keep us together if other forces drive us apart. Sacks argues that we need covenantal relationships, which generate trust. They rest on a shared commitment to ideas, issues, values and goals. They fill deep needs and they enable meaning and fulfillment. In a covenant, two parties come together to achieve what they can't achieve alone. In a process oriented understanding of disease and illness, we engage in a dialogue with aspects of our diversity that are expressed in our symptom experiences. We also join in a covenantal relationship with our body that is based on compassion and a belief in our common humanity. Process- and community-based medicine values diversity and the meaning in what we conventionally perceive as weak, ill, abnormal, etc. The Tao Te Ching says:

> I am a fool. Oh, yes! I am confused. Others are clear and bright, but I alone am dim and weak. Others are sharp and clever, but I alone am dull and stupid. Oh, I drift like the waves of the sea, without direction, like the restless wind. Everyone else is busy, but I alone am aimless and depressed. I am different. I am nourished by the great mother.

There is wisdom in success, intelligence, health and wellness—and there are other wisdoms in depression, weakness and illness. We need difference and diversity and awareness of the space and flow between the separate parts and opinions. The gifts of our vulnerabilities and imperfections, of our failings and illnesses, of our problems and conflicts are that they can bring us together and connect us with Jung's essential, the unbroken wholeness, and Uexküll's environing world. David Eagleman (2011) described our brains as a neural parliament with competing parties. But beyond the competing neural networks, beyond the separate parts, beyond the parallel worlds there is a unity and uniqueness.

The health-sickness and the healer-patient relationships are fundamental. Health and sickness, the healer and the ill, doctor and patient are basic human motifs. Both poles are inherent and potential forms of human experiences and behaviors and contained within the same individual. Many situations require the help of an external expert physician or healer, but no doctor can be effective without the patient's inner healer. A surgeon can stitch up a wound, but something in the injured person's body and psychology must help to heal.

Doctors and helpers are wounded healers and every patient and client has an inner doctor and knower. As patients we often hand our inner healer over to the physician and as providers we forget our own wounds and pains. When our patients and clients project their healing onto us as providers we might start to see ourselves as great helpers, the source of health and hope. We can help, heal, ease pain and give the patient meaning. Our clients and patients are lost without us. Ultimately this leads to us seeing patients as victims, poor, helpless and unreasonable. Our clients and patients start to rely on us to bring help, awareness and cure. Unconsciously they might stop complying with us and not follow our recommendations. They lose conscience of their own health.

If doctors are only healers and patients only victims, if we keep the health-sickness poles separate, the healthy remain one-sidedly strong and well and the sick weak and unwell. The sick become perennial patients and the healthy self-important, narrow-minded and blind to their own need for growth and development.

Health-in-sickness and sickness-in-health symbolizes that everyone has within them the health-sickness "archetype." We all are brothers and sisters in this shared human experience. And lastly, Rumi said that the light enters you at the wounded place and Cohen said that it gets in where there is a crack.

APPENDIX I

# *Dreambody Medicine Forum: Body Symptoms, Health and Community*

This is an annotated transcript of a class that I gave together with Dr. Jai Tomlin in Portland in Mai of 2013. The goal of the class was to link the individual experience of body symptoms with larger cultural and social issues. Participants had the opportunity to explore their own experience and learn the social aspects of illness through sharing their experiences in a group format. I am including this transcript in the appendix to convey a real life experience of the work with body symptoms both on an individual and collective level.

## *Introduction*

In her introduction Dr. Tomlin shared the history of previous Dreambody seminars called Lava Rock clinics. These clinics were two-week body symptom forums led by Dr. Arnold Mindell and Dr Max Schupbach. In these clinics Drs. Mindell and Schupbach worked with people with serious or chronic health issues and body symptoms.

Dr. Tomlin then acknowledged the fear and anxiety that come with having a body symptom. She shared her experience of symptoms being both the worst thing that one hate and something that can be meaningful. She suggested befriending that symptom and making it known to oneself rather than just pushing it away.

She described how Arnold Mindell developed the dreambody concept in the 1970's and quoted him saying: "The dreambody appears as sentient, generally unrecognized sensations that eventually manifest in dream images, body experiences and symptoms. The dreaming bridges the gap between our measurable physical bodies and the immeasurable experiences of the so-called mind. What we see in our dreams we feel in our bodies; likewise, what we experience in our bodies we can find in our dreams" (Mindell 1984). She explained that the Processwork approach to the "dreaming body" is not a cookbook method and that we don't assign specific meanings to specific symptoms such as low back pain means you have lack of support. People describe their pain in many ways. One person might say, "my pain is sharp or shooting;" another person could say, "dull, achy, throbbing or pressure."

She depicted Processwork and dreambody work as a therapeutic modality that tries to help people and relieve their suffering as well as following the clients' process and discover its "beauty", purpose and meaning. For her the Processwork paradigm is similar to what she finds in native cultures which see symptoms or worst problems as worthy opponents or allies. By wrestling with them one may find a certain type of power that is healing to one's soul.

She gave an example of her experiencing passing out. She found out that she had low blood pressure and anemia and that she needed to take iron. With Processwork she started to work on the dizzy state and found that it was an ally, something like a spiral galaxy. Through that experience she was able to get in touch with something that connected her with her feeling and intuitive nature. She concluded her introduction with describing dreambody work as an integration and evolution of various healing modalities, conventional and complementary ones, as well as shamanistic types of healing.

In my introduction I explored the social dimensions of health and dreambody work. I shared the Greek myth of Procrustes. Procrustes was an ogre who owned an inn on the way to Athens. Everybody who wanted to go to Athens and was on their way toward Athens had to stop at Procrustes' inn. Procrustes would feed people, give them dinner and keep them overnight. The problem with his inn was that it only had one size of bed. All the beds were the same size. Once you would go lie down and sleep at night, Procrustes would come into your room and if you were too short he would stretch you, and if you were too tall he would cut your limbs, your legs, to fit the size of the bed. And only then he would allow you to continue to go to Athens. You had to fit that one size bed.

I shared my views that we are all actually like Procrustes. We act like him on an everyday basis. We cut our legs to a certain size or we stretch ourselves to fit a certain mainstream idea of who we should be and who we are expected to be and how we are expected to behave. Especially if we want to fit into the mainstream of society. In the myth, social mainstream is represented by Athens, which was the metropolis and which is the symbol of mainstream. One aspect of the social dimension of health is that we want to fit in. We want to be part of the community. We want to behave like everybody else. We don't want to stand out. It could be dangerous. So we limit or stretch ourselves to conform. That might be a reason why sometimes we develop symptoms. We conform because of the values and morals that are part of the common experience of community.

There is another aspect of the ogre, which is also an important piece to the social dimensions of health: the social determinants. By that I mean the way we are as a community, the way we relate as a community, which has huge impacts on our bodies. All the social dynamics of let's say, skin color, gender, sexual orientation, or social dynamics that are based on economics and access to resources create what is called microaggressions, minor daily hassles that we experience sometimes consciously, sometimes subconsciously, subliminally. We feel them in the atmosphere of the social environment. These microaggressions have an impact on us and our bodies. They stress us. They put a stress load on us, which creates symptoms. These social dynamics determine why some people are more privileged and because of that privilege have more chance to stay healthy and why some people with fewer privileges in these different dimensions are more at risk.

I stressed the importance of looking at body symptoms from an individual and community perspective.

## *Demonstration*

Jai[61]: We thought we would demonstrate what we have been talking about. Pierre and I thought we would work with Vivian, who so courageously said she would volunteer.

(To Vivian) Where would you like to sit or stand or twirl?

Pierre: Are you shy?

Vivian: yes, I am.

Pierre: Who is going to eat you up? Who is the ogre?

61 To simplify I am using first person names for the facilitators. For confidentiality reasons I changed the name of the person who worked on her symptom.

Jai: We are a relatively nice group.

(To the group) We talked about that: what is being said in this individual work tonight stays in the group. Talk about the learning. But everything personal is confidential. Most people are aware of that.

Pierre: Shall we sit or stand? What is best for you?

Vivian: The floor looks good.

Jai: Let's get some cushions.

Vivian: The floor is fine.

Pierre: Hmmm, the hard floor. No comfort....[62]

Vivian: So we were going to chat for a few minutes. (Vivian takes her shoes off.)

Jai: Vivian, I am so glad you are here. Do you want to say anything about your symptom? What would you like to work on?

Vivian: Yes, well, I am excited to be here. Although, very nervous. Thanks for having me here. So, I was thinking of exploring my headaches. I don't have them lately. For the last months I had no headaches, but....

Jai: So you don't have one right now?

Vivian: No, which is good. But they were really painful. They were on the right side of the head.

Jai: Always?

Vivian: Yes, my left side was peaceful, and my right side was tense. It was always on the right side. The first time it happened was almost a year ago.

Jai: Do you remember that first episode? What were you doing?

Vivian: Yes, that first time.

Jai: You are smiling?

Vivian: I was sitting on the couch and suddenly my head started aching here and here (shows different parts on the right side of her head), very tense. I remember I went into the bedroom and I lied

62 I pick up on the fact that Vivian is comfortable on the hard floor and think there must be a part of her that wants to be tough and is possibly against comfort.

down. It was after a long, stressful time. And all my right side got kind of numb.

Jai: How long did it last?

Vivian: The intense pain was something about 15 minutes, but then I was very dizzy for two hours, maybe because of the intense pain. I had to go to the hospital and I usually don't go to the hospital.

Jai: It was so bad. How was your blood pressure?

Vivian: It was good.

Pierre: What did they say in the hospital?[63]

Vivian: Well, they didn't exactly know, but they did some tests. First they told me that it was related to the trigeminal nerve. They sent me home and asked me to do some tests. I did an MRI, which was fine. But then it came back. Sometimes the headaches were lasting all night. I couldn't sleep. First they said it was the trigeminal nerve. So I had very intense pain here and also my eye and jaw. All this area (shows the trigeminal nerve area). The headaches would keep me awake all night, they were very intense.

Jai: What would be most helpful to you? If you could ask for help in a certain area, what would be the best thing that could happen this evening?

Vivian: (thinking)

Pierre: You had an idea....

Vivian: I was just thinking what you were talking about before, about how exploring a symptom could relate to something bigger than yourself.

Pierre: Greece was in a difficult situation, and still is. You said you had a very stressful time. I was wondering if you could say some words about the context. What kind of stress, if it is okay to say.

Vivian: There was generally a lot of tension in the atmosphere. I had a lot of relationship problems at that time.

Pierre: Social difficulties and then relationship stuff.

Vivian: Social aspects, relationship stuff, all very grrr... (Makes a face and growling sound).

---

63 In this first part Jai and I are exploring the medical aspects of her symptoms, making sure that Vivian is taking care of her symptoms medically and not neglecting this important consensus reality aspect.

Pierre: Right (laughter), not just peaceful.[64]

Vivian: Yep.

Jai: I never had migraines.

Vivian: Yes, they said it may be migraines.

Jai: And so I am not exactly sure what that feels like. I get a little headache once in a while. I know it is different because I treat people with severe headaches. I am trying to get a sense of how they felt from you. And maybe you could create the pain to me or maybe if you are too shy you can show me on a pillow. What is it like to have a headache?[65]

Vivian: (hesitates)

Pierre: Maybe because they are too tense you don't want to hurt Jai?

Vivian: Yeah, they are too much.

Jai: Maybe on my arm. (Vivian grabs Jai's arm). Oh, it's actually a twisting thing. (Vivian continues to twist the skin on Jai's forearm.)

Vivian: Okay (makes a growling sound), grr.

Jai: And you are making a sound with that.

Vivian: (Continues) Grr.

Jai: Good job.

Pierre: Oh, wow.

Jai: (Gives Vivian a pillow to amplify the twisting motion.)

Pierre: Really go for it.

Vivian: Grr.

Jai: Are you okay physically?

Vivian: Yeah.

Jai: Wondering if you could make a drawing.

---

64 I validate the themes that Vivian described in her head experiences: one side being peaceful and the other tense.

65 Jai is asking Vivian to recreate the somatic symptom experience on her to get a better sense of the quality of that symptom.

Pierre: Just do it a little more with the pillow. So you know what it's all about. If you could really go for it, and then we can do the drawing (Vivian continues to twist the pillow.)[66]

Vivian: It is more like drilling.

Pierre: Use your whole body and just do it.

Jai: Yeah.

Pierre: Yes, grr[67].

Vivian: Grr. It is squeezing like squeezing an orange (laughs).

Pierre: (Makes a loud grr sound, then to Vivian) You are looking at me. Who is that? What kind of character is that?

Vivian: Grr... (Squeezes and drills the cushion)

Jai: That is more than a squeeze. That is a squeeze with a something. You want to try to stand and do that with your whole body?

Vivian: Grr.

Pierre: Yeah, I saw that. Grr.

Vivian: Grr. (keeps squeezing and drilling the cushion and hesitates at the same time)

Pierre: Yeah... Ready for a big squish?

Jai: That looks pretty good. Is there something that doesn't like that?

Pierre: It's not very peaceful.

Vivian: It's not very peaceful, it's not very friendly.

Pierre: You should be a gentle, friendly woman[68].

Vivian: Grr (loudly)!

Jai: Are there any words that go along with that?

Vivian: (Looks at Jai intensely)

Pierre: There was a little threat in there.

---

66 Vivian appears to be on an edge to express the energy of the symptom more forcefully. I was thinking that changing from movement into drawing would allow her to avoid going further and miss the process. On the other hand Vivian might have expressed her experience in a drawing equally well.

67 I am joining Vivian in expressing the quality of her symptoms by matching her energy and supporting her in unfolding her process.

68 I am taking the other side to give it a contrast.

Jai: Good thing.

Pierre: Yeah, you can go for it. You are someone to reckon with, no? Maybe you should be peaceful, no?

Jai: Just sitting on the couch, relaxed.

Vivian: No!

Pierre: Yes! No, what? Well, it is a beginning. It is a no. No to what? No to being... (Vivian shows some feelings) You have a lot of feelings about it, too.

Vivian: I am not going to sit on the couch!

Pierre: There is a lot of power. I got you.

Jai: Just sitting on the couch it's a stressful thing. No. There's something you are supposed to do?

Vivian: Take the most out of it!

Pierre: I did hear that. Get the most out of it, to get to the bottom, to the core. (Vivian shows some more feelings.) You have feelings about it?

Vivian: Some, yes, to actually have permission to go for it.

Pierre: To have the permission to really go for it...

Vivian: Everything.

Pierre: Everything, to the core, everything, got it. What stops you? I mean, obviously I can imagine a lot of things that stop you. But what *stops* you?

Vivian: What stops me is CR sometimes. Everyday reality and I don't trust myself.

Pierre. You don't trust yourself. Now this other one doesn't have any problem with trust, I'd say. It doesn't care about anybody else. It just goes. (Laughter)

Vivian: Right, it just goes for it. It's just warming up.

Jai: How about if you could observe us acting both sides out? To change levels might be helpful.

Pierre: Okay, grr. (Role playing[69])

Jai: No.

---

69 Jai and I are role playing the inner conflict and debate while Vivian is observing us.

Pierre: What do you mean?

Jai: So nice sitting on the couch.

Pierre: No, you can't relax.

Jai: Stop it already. I want to relax. I am having relationship problems. Oh. My god the country...

Pierre: There is no time for it. Just shut up. Shut up. It's time to grrr.

Jai: Oh, my head. I can't stand that.

Pierre: (To Vivian) Feel free to take a side[70].

Pierre: I've had enough of just sitting around. There is no time to waste. Everything is upheaval. They need me. I need to get involved.

Jai: Why do you have to be so twisty about it and drilling and chaotic and painful?

(To Vivian): You are smiling?

Pierre: You are holding me back. All these conventions.

Jai: I am holding you back. I am.

Pierre: Yes, sure you are.

Jai: I am?

Pierre: Yes, obviously.

Jai: Oh. (Laughter) How am I holding you back?

Vivian: (Talking to Jai and Pierre) Um... Jai, you asked something at some point. Why do you have to be so twisty about it, and squeezy?

Jai: Yes.

Vivian: I mean, there is a communication problem here.

Pierre: There is a communication problem?

Jai: Yes. Yeah, there is.

Pierre: So?

Vivian: (Addressing Jai) He (Pierre) is becoming twisty because you are not. You are relaxing there and not paying enough attention! So...

---

70 I am offering her to step in and help us with both or any sides.

Jai: Yeah, but...

Vivian: (To Pierre) And she is relaxing there because you are not paying enough attention, too. (To Jai and Pierre) You need some rest and you need some action, right. But you have to let each other know.

Jai: How are we going to do that? I don't like him very much. Too twisty, squishy.

Pierre: I don't like her that much, too. I feel constrained by her.

Vivian: None of you can get out into the world alone.

Pierre: I see, if I go on my own I can't...

Vivian: You can't do that. You're going to get hurt. You need each other.

Pierre: Right.

Jai: (To Vivian) Do you have a tip of how we could do that? I don't want to sit on the couch only.

Pierre: No, you are just holding me back.

Jai: If you go out there and twist around you are going to hurt yourself.

Pierre: I can't. I feel so held back, pleasing and peaceful and everything around me goes crazy and I need to go into the world.

Jai: Yeah, but you need some of that peace.

Pierre: Grr!

Jai: You can't only be grr all the time.

Vivian: I have a very simple way. Just let each other know what you need. Let each other know what you are doing there. It's like, let each other know.

Jai: How should we let each other know?

Vivian: (To Pierre) Like let her know what you are going after and why you're doing that and what it is that you want to do. (To Jai) And also let him know what you need. Set a timeframe together: I am going to rest for that much. I am going to go out in the world to do this... and everything can happen.

Pierre: Ok.

Vivian: Don't fight.

Jai: Talk to each other about it. Yeah, great.

Pierre: (To Vivian) You are thinking...

Vivian: Makes sense. Wow. It makes sense. I am thinking that lots of times I'm just doing nothing and then I am getting very anxious and critical of myself for doing nothing, then I am not letting myself know that this is my time to do nothing and later I will do something. Then my other part gets really grr.

Jai: These two parts dance together. Not only fighting, but talking, negotiating.

Pierre: It is interesting in a way that your process appears initially as a hesitation or reluctance to bring out all your power and strength and to really come out with your grr. Initially, it looks as if you need support to bring that out. But it is also a relationship process between a part of you that needs peace and relaxation and a part of you that wants to be active in the world. And you described that split in the two experiences of your head, one very peaceful and calm and the other with the ache. There is a relationship conflict between these two sides and how to bring awareness to these two tendencies and get them to know each other.

Vivian: You can't get out of either world.

Jai: You can't get out of either world. Got to befriend those two. Let's take it one little step further and see how that could be helpful for you, and is that at all helpful in the larger community? Would that be helpful when you go back home to Greece? Such a tough scene there.

Vivian: The first thing that comes to mind is how amongst my community in Greece we tend to blame each other for not doing what each one of us thinks is best. Not out there enough. Many people can go out on the streets and other people need to stay and care, need to garden. Doing different things. We don't appreciate the diversity, thinking we all have to do the same thing in the same way.

Pierre: If you do too much advocacy, you might get hopeless. But it needs both.

Vivian: Thank you so much.

Pierre: Good luck in Greece.

Vivian: Thanks, everybody.

Pierre: We can see how the field in Greece creates this pressure for social action.

Jai: But it also changed us in the room, just now.

Pierre: Maybe there is some feedback or comments.

Erin[71]: One of the things to think about: giving and not receiving, and how a part of me tends to go out of balance. Filling up your cup and relaxing, needing to relax. If fits with the left and right brains, the giving and receiving sides of the body.

David: Thank you so much. The thing you were working on was very profound, and I felt deeply what you were doing.

Frank: Jai and Pierre, you modeled patience. You explored. You just held the space. Patient, witnessing. Didn't push, elicited. Unfolding her initial headache into something simple.

Dawn: I'd just like to make a comment as someone who used to get a lot of migraines. That was like seeing an aspect of myself. I have worked on it personally a lot internally and with help. It was not until the inside story of what the headache was about, it being connected about being a minority group, until I connected to the rage of homophobia that my migraines diminished. It was a huge wake-up call and it may have nothing to do with you, Vivian. But, I mean, you're living in Greece. How could you not be affected by the turbulence? It really woke me up. It changed the way I did my work with people. Alone in a room with people is good work. But if that is not connected to the larger culture, larger system, I now believe that is limited. That was a wonderful reflection of how those energies are not separate. Thank you.

Peter: Thank you for doing that work and facilitating. I also struggled with headaches.

Pierre: Oh, that is pretty frequent. How many have headaches? (Many participants put their hands up)

Miriam: I felt very touched at one point. It was something to do with the persistence of that energy. V, you said: "I'm only just warming up." It's a power and I also was thinking of social change. It doesn't happen overnight. It happens over a long time. I have to appreciate the persistence because you don't see the results imme-

71 To keep it confidential I changed the names of the participants.

diately. To appreciate the sticking with something. That capacity of not giving up. Very touching.

Pierre: Well, maybe it's time for a break.

## *Forum*

(Participants met first in small groups of 4 to give everybody the chance to speak. The facilitators posed the question: How does gender play a role in Vivian's process or not?)

Pierre: Let us start with reporting what you discussed in your small groups or what was important for you and then see how we as a group can go deeper into a discussion. Let us start with one or two people. Share what was important for you. And let's see where it goes. Who wants to start?

Erin: Not me.

Nina: In our small group conversation we discussed the topic of femininity and Greekness. We were saying the center was so lucky to have Greek women students. One is a member of parliament. Yes, very impressive. Greek feminine energy. And this goddess energy coming from Greece. Lesbianism from Lesbos. Elevation of goddesses. Part of Western civilization. Cool that we have a lot of Greek female students.

Pierre: I'm just noticing. Feminine powers, definitely.

Joe: I'm a little bit jaw dropping at what Nina said. Wow. Shocked. So cool. Western European centric. Greece is a symbol of a place and a country.

Bill: Slightly on that note, one of the things I noticed was I joined a group that was all Asian men. I was remarking on that and I felt slightly guilty but then also felt, how often does this happen to me? Not that often. Then we got other kinds of racial diversity.

Jai: It is good to see you here. So that just kind of spontaneously happened.

Bill: Well, I saw Fred and we were talking...

Pierre: Greek women and Asian men. They should get together. (Laughter) Hot spot.[72]

Amy: Ah, it's Interesting. In our group we also talked about gender. I was in a group with Alice and Caroline. We had two roles, one role that said... (Turning to Caroline) do you want to say how it was?

Caroline: The question was about gender, right. How is gender part of Vivian's process or not? It kind of defined a female and male energy and what in general we think about them or how they're represented. I got in a bit of trouble because I stereotyped it: like, typical feminine energy is soft, gentle, maybe mother earth energy and male energy is powerful, out there, the tough one. It is also represented in the yin and yang symbol and the symbol also shows how the different energies flow together—how a little of female energy is in male and male energy in female. We were curious how Vivian was identifying, as more female or male.

Amy: So that was one role (laughter) and the other role was: I am following an experience I don't know. It is my experience. I don't know if it belongs to a gender and it is something that I am feeling inside. And we had a heated interaction around something saying this is how things are, male and female, and something else that says: I am not sure. I am just exploring something.

Daryl: Gender is a very tricky question. That came up in our group. In the process of Vivian we saw a very active and very passive role, not explicitly gender-based. The discussion goes right into stereotypes of that. In Yoga, right is masculine and left is feminine. This is problematic and limited in contrast to just being curious about the process. Gender is very tricky to talk about.

Alice: I felt most of us would have both elements too, but not necessarily gender specific.

Fiona: (To Alice) I liked that you were saying there is feminine and masculine energy within everyone. In our group we talked about this idea of the being and the doing. The feminine being and the masculine doing. It is one thing that we heard in Vivian's process that gardening was less important than marching in the street and

72 Hot spots are moments of intense group feedback such as strong emotional reactions or many side conversations. They point at important dynamics and are worth holding for the group to develop more awareness.

fighting. And how oppression makes the feminine less important than the masculine. (To the group) This is something we didn't talk about, yet.

Pierre: (Some participants are raising their hands) Please feel free to speak out.

Gerald: (Addressing the two facilitators Jai and Pierre): Literally you two acted it out. There was the masculine (Pierre) doing the more acting, the feminine (Jai) was more passive. That was interesting

Heather: There is also the right brain and the left brain.

Pierre: (Speaking to Gerald) I actually noticed that myself. I noticed that I went a bit further in bringing out and unfolding the active wrestling piece of Vivian's work.

Lilly: I had a very strange experience during Vivian's process. As you were working, my right eye started hurting inside. I had to close it because I felt pain and this is my instinctual reaction. My strong side is my right side, which goes out and does things. And my left side is quieter. When I closed my right eye I realized how that eye had to stay inside in order for the other to go out. I wonder if by closing the right eye the amount of power of the strong part relaxes and the weak part is able to go out. They are just different energies. Changing roles makes space for another kind of strength. The strong one relaxes and the soft goes out.

Erin: I would like to live in that kind of society. Where the rigid polarities are more blurred. I like that very much. Just a comment.

Pierre: On the other hand there is another side in which there is more division between these two polarities.

Erin: On this side we don't want to be held to the contents of either polarity; masculine equals extraverted, feminine is yin or introverted. Maybe this side is rebelling, maybe it is dreaming. Something else has to happen. Maybe it's time for a new attitude or approach.

Lucas: I experience things differently. For me, for example, sitting on the couch is powerful even though it is seen as not powerful. It can be powerful to be needy, and sensitive is powerful. Relaxing and just being is very powerful.

Erin: I think that is beautiful and for me that is part of what I see beginning to try and happen in the Greek culture with all the turbulence and challenges that are happening. A different way of communicating wants to happen. Dropping expectations and not setting anyone up. The normal forms of communication are breaking.

Nina: We don't have to all be the same. This is my hope for America, something about plurality.

Pierre: Is there a role or a side that says this is not good enough? We need to be more active, go out with our strength; we are not really in support of that more quiet power?

Lucas: I was just thinking there is a side that says this active, outgoing power is also valid, it is not only bad. To value both more.

Erin: (Stepping into a role) Yes, says quiet power we are not really interested in fighting with extraverted power. I don't want to do to you what you have done to me.

Pierre: That is a strong statement. It refers to a historical put down. That is an aspect of the process. Someone might speak to that.

Alice: (Addressing Pierre) Well, I wondered why the question was asked. What did you see that suggested that gender might be part of Vivian's process? Why did you see it that way? Well, I could get more angry about it. How come!?

Pierre: You are right. There is an implicit put down. I agree, when I thought of the question I wasn't aware of it. By asking the question I implicitly put women down. You are right to challenge me.

Nina: But there is diversity in that. I appreciate it. The acknowledgement.

Pierre: This is an interesting moment: someone directly challenging me.

Erin: I would like you, Alice, to say more. What is it that makes you irritated about the question of gender? Because you might be speaking for more people than you think.

Alice: Oh, okay. There was a lot in Vivian's process. Obviously there were oppositional polarities or yin and yang, differences that were involved in a bit of a struggle, but I didn't see gender as part of that. I can be as strong and oppositional as most men. Any of them, you, and I think you (speaking to Pierre) could be tender and gardening (laughter). I bet you can cook, too. I could be as outraged as you and you can be as angry as me, as well. It's not particularly a gender thing, is it? I mean I dare you. (Laughter)

Joseph: Gender, because Pierre is sexist for interpreting it that way.

Pierre: I agree with you. It is implicit; there is an indirect put down. I asked the question because I know migraines are more frequent in women, from a medical point of view. And I think there is a relationship between migraine and sexism and the put down of women's power. I do agree with you that by asking the question I am putting women down.

Alice: Historically, madness was identified as women's problems. The majority of people who were put in the asylums were women. I didn't really see it as part of Vivian's process. And I love how you speak. Thank you, Pierre, because you really take the wind out of my sails.

Heather: Your interaction is: is it this? Is it that? Don't label my process, my experience beyond my gender role. Oh, I need words to describe what I see. I don't want to be labeled in any way. I think those are two roles.

Fiona: I was curious because we do have separate genders in society. We do have women and we do have men and others. I am not too familiar with Greek culture. I was wondering if there maybe more dominance by men in Greek culture. If you evolve as a woman in a culture where male dominance is pervasive, women might begin to manifest symptoms of the pathology inherent in that imbalance. Does that make sense? So, I was wondering if there is actual credence or truth to looking at gender in a symptom. Associating the two to look back at a manifestation of a cultural problem.

Nina: I am still on the other side here. I like it that you think about these things. It is not often that you hear a man talk about it.

Amy: It is interesting. I am really having to work on myself. I have so much feeling around this. Why, why? It is so painful. Why can't I just experience myself? Why must you need to tell me what it is? And tell me that I can't experience it because it doesn't belong to my gender? I am so much larger than this body.

Erin: You don't want to be put in a box based on gender.

Amy: Why can't you see my nature? What is wrong with that?

Erin: Can I try and answer?

Pierre: Good, there is someone on the other side.

Erin: There is nothing wrong with your gender. There is nothing wrong with you wanting to tell me not to see you only through gendered eyes. I have held on to gender constructions in order to make sense of the universe because I don't often really understand people, and sometimes having this box called male and female gives a little polarity. But, I appreciate the reminder not to make this box a prison for anyone else. So I thank you for that. Gender distinctions are fine but they are limited. I get it. There might be other views here but I am representing one of them.

Amy: I am sure there are other views here.

Erin: Well, maybe there is one more conservative who says the world is made of males and females and there are some people in between and beyond but the main story is men and women. What's the problem?

Pierre: (Helping Erin's role go further) And we want women to stay at home and we want them to be... Well, this is an unpopular viewpoint...

Erin: Yes, and I want my man to go out and work and bring the bacon home.

Pierre: I want the woman to be gentle and peaceful and at home.

Erin: And as a man. I'll go out, and I'll bring it in. I will keep her in comfort and take care of the kids. Without that the world will fall apart. If you take apart the heterosexual family unit we're all.

Gerald: (Representing another viewpoint) Yeah, but what about me? I was mother, father, everything to my child. I had to be both. I couldn't be just one. I was both and I didn't stop to think am I being masculine now or feminine. No, I just was.

Joseph: (Responding to Gerald and reinforcing Erin's viewpoint) Yeah, that is because you are confused. Men decide everything about family. That is how it works. Then there is less confusion.

Pierre: (Speaking to Erin and Joseph) It is hard to be on that side, difficult to speak out from that perspective.

Alice: It would help me to know actually what is so important for you over there (addressing Erin and Joseph) about being so... like, why are you so attached to that?

Erin: Structure, order, prediction, the human race continuing.

Alice: Is it really continuing? I mean look around at what is happening.

Joseph: Population growth is one of the worst problems.

Alice: Is that really working for you? How is it working for you? Are you happy over there?

Erin: It is interesting. In this role I notice two directions. I don't want to talk personally. I just want to bring out my dogma and spray it: the values of the regular structure of male and female and the family unit, because I don't want to talk about my personal life.

Gerald: Same thing. Saying this is how the family should be. Traditionality is a good thing.

Erin: We are traditionalists.

Joseph: In my view marriage is between one male and one female.

Pierre: Ouch.

Alice: You can't be a little more creative than that? Come on. Have a bit more Technicolor over here. It is a little limited. I want to be able to express myself.

Joseph: How dare you attack my family. It is you people who want to...

Alice: You people. Do not talk about me as you people. I mean, really. I am sorry if you hear it that way. I respect your family. I love your family. I do not want to destroy your family.

Erin: That is genuine.

Alice: I am sorry that you see it that way. That is not my agenda. I want to be able to be myself. I want to be an individual and not the same as everybody else.

Joseph: Yeah, I was worried about my family. I want people to be kind and good and moral and follow God and to know what God's plan is for them.

Susie: (Speaking to Joseph) I have a question. Just for my clarification, are you speaking as a role?

Joseph: Yes, as a role.

Susie: Alice, you are speaking half personally. So I think here we have to be sensitive. (To Joseph) It is most likely not what you would stand for, so I just want to hold you both, so no one gets hurt. And there is a role in society...

Alice: Very powerful, and I wonder you know what people who are traditionalist think. Maybe they have a high dream. A beautiful high dream.

Joseph: I notice that I started to feel scared.

Amy: Yes, there is a lot of power over here. It is true. And it is just the beginning. I was thinking there is a lot of power in the emotion. There is a lot of emotion on this side. And fear.

Alice: I feel I've got to come out strongly to be heard. There are so many of you. And tradition is so structured and safe.

Amy: Institutionalized.

Alice: I want to be more creative and more open.

Amy: You just want to be yourself.

Erin: That is the point of connection between the two sides. That's how you are the same.

Vivian: This might sound scary. I need to say this from a very deep feeling place. From a high dream for myself, too. It is not coming from a need to destroy. It is coming from a deep need to live. Coming from a very sensitive place. Very vulnerable. Yes, it is the same experience. I feel like my efforts to know myself individually are inherently threatening. If I try to be myself I am threatening their sanity. Threatening the people who depend on structure. And it is hard enough being in this space on the path to self discovery.

Amy: (Addressing the traditionalist side) And our family over here is dying. I need your help. There are children who are dying in schools for being different. There is drug addiction in the communities. I need you to help deal with being different because of the structures that are being upheld. We need your help. It is not only your family that needs to stay alive and thrive.

Joseph: We do help. We have charities that give away food, and God's love is there for everyone.

Pierre: We are shifting levels; there is power in your own diversity. There is a personal level and a more social or cultural level between different roles. I don't know if there is one side that hasn't spoken yet. I am trying to feel it in myself. I might feel threatened by my own inner diversity.

Amy: Thank you. That's relieving.

Pierre: There is a part of me that is really scared believing and trusting in my own diversity. I'd rather forget about it and go by social roles. It is scary to trust myself. Do you know what I mean? I'd rather forget about it. Don't want to look at my own strengths and power. I'd rather just live, because it is too scary. I do have that. So maybe there is an aspect of that on this side. It needs a little of something conservative to hold on to. It is scary, to feel that.

We also have to take care of the time. I don't know if that is a good moment to stop or if there is something else that needs to happen.

Vivian: Time to relax and garden.

Gerald: Such an appealing idea.

Joseph: (Responding to Amy asking for help) A little curious. That side needed help. What kind of help?

Amy: I mean that right here is a good beginning. It would be helpful if you reflected on your power and rank. You have a lot of institutionalized power as well, which is really oppressive.

Joseph: (To Amy) Your side has a lot of power as well, amazing diversity and wildness and creativity.

Amy: (To Joseph) I love that you asked how that side could be helped In a way that was genuine and not patronizing. Turns out that as a gay man I can go out and ask for help and advice.

Joseph: Yes, you also have power. Maybe you can lead something, that's what I felt.

Pierre: There are a lot of teachers.

Michael: I just noticed something about the origin of the word weird, a Welsh word, which meant to have a foot in two different worlds, to bridge the two. The priests used to wear frocks. It started as a way to integrate the feminine. They knew that the only real way to God was to integrate.

Erin: Right and maybe on that note we could weirdly end, knowing that we are working on having one foot in this world and one in this other. Two poles, one in contact with the other. And we need both for our own wholeness.

Pierre: Obviously that discussion is not finished and needs to be continued. But maybe that is a good time to stop. Thank you all for a lively and deep discussion.

## APPENDIX II

# *Health-In-Sickness Toolkit*

The practical tools I recommend here are suggestions. Please amend them with your own ideas and knowledge. Some recommendations address the consensus reality (CR) aspects of your "small" health process; some are suggestions for helping you to connect with your "big health" or "dreaming" (NCR) process. I also added ideas for providers and caregiver teams. The exercises are not meant to replace consulting a therapist or medical doctor.

## *Practical Tools for Current and Future Patients*

### Creative Wellness Checklist[73]

Health: A sustainable relationship between you, your "dreaming" process and the meanings your symptoms are bringing to your awareness. Symptoms are processes you need to pick up on even if they go away.

Medicine and health are multidimensional processes. They include:

#### Allopathic and Complementary Medical Procedures

- □ Am I adhering to the medical procedures of my culture?

73 Checklists and health risk assessments are popular tools for helping individuals "manage" their wellness and health. They help us become more aware of wellness areas that need our attention. They are based on a mainstream consensus about what is considered to contribute to wellness and good health. They fail to take into account the complexity of the wellness and health related issues and implicitly assume that everybody has the same opportunity and privilege to engage in safe exercise, eat healthy, have good relationships etc... They also one-sidedly presume that health means being slim, fit, in a loving relationship etc... These hidden assumptions disregard the diversity and rank aspects of health and are therefore inflammatory. Most of the questions in this checklist address health behaviors and as such they are incomplete.

- ☐ Did I have my regular preventive health checks/ screenings (i.e., PAP smear, mammogram, annual checkup with my primary care doctor, cholesterol check, blood pressure check and dental cleaning)?
- ☐ Do I take my prescribed medications and herbs as they've been prescribed?

**Diet**

- ☐ Did I eat a healthy breakfast (i.e., high fiber, low sugar, fresh fruit, and good protein)?
- ☐ Am I following an anti-inflammatory diet (i.e., including vegetables, fruits, beans, deep sea fish, shitake mushrooms and green tea)?
- ☐ Did I take my supplements to complement what I don't get in my diet (i.e., a good multi vitamin, fish oil, vitamin C, antioxidants, Co-Q-10)?
- ☐ Did I eat healthy snacks (i.e., fresh fruit, raw nuts)?
- ☐ Did I avoid high-sugar carbohydrates after 2 pm and especially in the evening before I go to bed (i.e., anything with flour, refined sugar or high fructose corn syrup)?[74]
- ☐ Did I read at least one food label today and learn from it?
- ☐ Did I get five to seven servings of vegetables in my diet?
- ☐ Did I drink 50-70 oz of water?
- ☐ Did I eat a healthy dinner with my family if possible (i.e., lean protein with veggies, interacting and listening to family)?
- ☐ Did I exercise self-compassion?[75]

---

74 Carbohydrates act as the primary source of fuel for the body, but you do not need to fuel your body before going to sleep. Snack on lean protein, veggies and natural peanut butter. If you must take in carbohydrates, have some fresh berries, which are low-glycemic and have a potent fat-burning effect.

75 Self-compassion is a significant ingredient in every diet and weight-loss plan; self-discipline, deprivation and neglect foster self-criticism and are counterproductive (Jean Fain, 2011)."

## Exercise

- ☐ Did I exercise or plan to today (i.e., try 30 minutes of interval cardio training and 45 minutes of yoga or strength training, while being mindful of intensity level)? Have I looked at myself naked in the mirror to know why?[76]

## Relaxation and Sleep Hygiene

- ☐ Did I practice (4-7-8) breathing? (Inhale for a count of four hold for a count of seven and exhale for a count of eight. Repeat five times and complete twice a day.)
- ☐ Did I drink something or do something to soothe my body before sleep (i.e., drinking chamomile or other herbal tea, reading something light, practicing meditation)?
- ☐ Did I work in 90-minute intervals and take breaks in between? Did I eat my lunch outside the office and seek some renewal?[77]
- ☐ Did I go to bed at a time that will allow me to get seven to nine hours of sleep?
- ☐ Do I follow the natural ups and downs of my energy level, use my fatigue or burnout feelings to relax, go inside and follow my dreaming?

## Intellectual Stimulation

- ☐ Did I feed and challenge my brain? Use it or lose it! (Challenging or stimulating activities include: reading;

---

76 Behavioral strategies recommend an emotional component to any change in health behavior. Looking in the mirror and seeing yourself naked can remind you what you want to achieve and why. This "shaming" strategy might motivate some people. On the other hand it disregards the whole issues of body image, eating disorders and shame. If it encourages your inner critic it is not helpful.

77 A new and growing body of multidisciplinary research shows that strategic renewal—including daytime workouts, short afternoon naps, longer sleep hours, more time away from the office and longer, more frequent vacations—boosts productivity, job performance and, of course, health.

completing a crossword puzzle; learning or teaching a new skill; and spending time with friends, family and social groups such as a reading club, bridge club, community learning center, etc.)

### Addictive Tendencies

- □ Am I aware of my addictive tendencies?
- □ Can I let loose and follow my altered states to connect with my creativity and spirituality?

### Dreaming, Night Dreams and Childhood Dreams

- □ Am I connected with my dreams and childhood myth?[78]

### Life Goals

- □ Why am I here? Is there something I would like to do?[79]

### Environment (Allergies, Atmospheres, Radiation)

- □ Is my home environment free of toxins, chemical pollutants, radon, mold, toxic relationships, etc.?
- □ What are the social issues I don't want to talk about?[80]

---

78 Staying connected with your dreaming process is powerful (preventive) medicine. Take time to remember your night dreams and share them with your loved ones. Meditate on your body experiences and step into their world, don't just fight them. Many of us had recurring early childhood dreams. These can show you some patterns and themes that will accompany you throughout your lifetime.

79 When you are in an unstable health situation it can be a matter of life and death to be connected with your purpose in life.

80 The social issues (gender, economic, power and rank, etc.) we repress can pollute our environments. They fester in our relationships and provide a background noise of hassles and stresses that have a strong impact on our bodies.

### Relationships

- □ Did I love someone or serve someone or something today?[81]

### Spiritual

- □ Is there something bigger than myself that pulls me?
- □ Did I wake up with an "attitude of gratitude" and ask what am I grateful for?[82]

### Body Mass Index, Cholesterol Levels and Blood Pressure

- □ What is my Body Mass Index? [83]
- □ What is my cholesterol level?[84]
- □ What is my blood pressure?[85]

### What to Ask Your Doctor When Diagnosed[86]

- □ What is my condition or diagnosis?
- □ What treatment do you recommend?

  A procedure or surgery

  A laboratory test or diagnostic (such as x-ray or MRI)

  A medication

---

81 Contributing to our families and our community keeps us connected and increases our "social capital." This in turn has beneficial health effects.

82 Not everybody and nobody can be grateful all the time. A spiritual connection is powerful medicine. See the earth dreaming exercise/meditation below as one possible simple way to connect to a spiritual realm.

83 Body Mass Index (BMI) is a number calculated from your weight and height. BMI is used as a screening tool to identify possible weight problems. For adults, a BMI below 18.5 is considered underweight, 18.5 – 24.9 normal, 25.0 – 29.9 overweight and 30.0 and above as obese.

84 For reference values check http://www.mayoclinic.com/health/cholesterol-levels/CL00001

85 For more information see http://en.wikipedia.org/wiki/Blood_pressure

86 If these questions feel difficult to ask, take someone with you to your doctor's appointment that can support you.

A therapy

- ☐ Why do you recommend the treatment?
- ☐ What are the results that you have achieved with the treatment?
- ☐ Do I need a particular treatment right away or are there less intense therapies that can be tried first?
- ☐ Are there lifestyle changes that may help my condition?
- ☐ What alternative approaches are there for my treatment?
- ☐ What is the price of the treatment?
- ☐ Was this test done previously?
- ☐ If so, what is the indication for repeating it? Is the result of a repeated test likely to be substantively different from the last result?
- ☐ If it was done recently elsewhere, can you get the result instead of repeating the test?
- ☐ Will the test result change my care?
- ☐ What are the probabilities and potential adverse consequences of a false positive test result?
- ☐ Am I in potential danger over the short term if I do not perform this test?
- ☐ Am I getting the test primarily because I've asked for it or is it to reassure me or you?[87]
- ☐ Are there other strategies to reassure me that are safer and less risky? How about I trust your opinion without the need for tests?

87 If you feel you need reassurance or you feel the doctor feels pressured to reassure you, you might want to take time to discuss your fears with your doctor. If this feels difficult, bring someone with you that can support you asking these questions.

## Using a Ulysses Contract[88] to Change Behavior

In Homer's Odyssey, Ulysses orders his men to securely lash him to the mast of the ship to prevent him from succumbing to the devastating lure of the beautiful Sirens' song. We can make our own behavioral contracts to offset the harmful actions we know our future selves will engage in, such as succumbing to cravings and other addictive impulses. Our brains are wired to be seduced by the short term. Voluntary controls and good intentions are insufficient to win over the short-term benefit. Therefore, we have to make deals with the "devil" and bind our future behavior. Here are some basic behavioral tips to control addictive behaviors:

- □ Minimize temptation and get rid of easy access to addictive substances. Avoid circumstances and situations that trigger the addictive behavior.
- □ Put money on the line: Make a deal/bet with someone that binds you financially[89].
- □ Recruit positive social or peer pressure[90].
- □ Involve positive and negative emotions[91].
- □ Establish new habits[92].

## Improving Placebo Exercises and Tools

Following mindfulness exercises give you some ideas about how to use your awareness to help you with moving forward toward big health.

---

88 I am thankful to David Eagleman for pointing towards this behavioral contract. For more information please see: David Eagleman, *Incognito, The Secret Lives of the Brain* (New York, NY: Pantheon Books, 2011).

89 Here are some examples of websites that help you lose weight by negotiating a business deal with your future self: HealthyWage.com, DietBet.com, gym-pact.com and stickk.com.

90 Joining an exercise group of like-minded friends/peers and attending AA or NA meetings are examples how you can both access emotional support and some positive challenge.

91 Seeing yourself in the mirror, for example, reminds you why you want to lose weight. Grant yourself a pleasurable gift for achieving a goal.

92 To change a habit and make a lifestyle change you need to invest seven weeks. In your action plan, choose one habit at a time and stick with it for seven weeks.

### Subtle Body Movement Tendency

1. Sit comfortably in a chair so that your upper body is able to move freely.
2. Relax, close your eyes and let yourself be moved.
3. Notice the subtle direction your body wants to move and let it take you where it wants.
4. Follow the movement until you experience some sort of resolution.
5. Let that resolution explain itself to you.

### Unfolding a Body Symptom

1. Think about one of your current symptoms, or a symptom you had in the past that you would like to understand better.
2. Where is or was the symptom located in your body? What does or did the symptom feel like?
3. Express the symptom energy with a gesture or hand motion. Sketch that energy on a piece of paper and call it *x energy*.
4. Now think about what part in you is against or disturbed by this energy. Feel into that part of you and make a gesture or hand motion that captures this experience. Sketch that energy on a piece of paper and call it *y energy*.
5. For advanced students or practitioners, make the hand motion for x with your left hand and the hand motion for y with your right hand and let both hands with their energies dance together until they find some resolution (something in you will feel resolved). Meditate on that third state.

### Energy Sketch on Pill or Medicine Bottle

As described in chapter III, draw the sketches of your *x* and *y energies* on your pill or medicine bottles. Do the same with your herbal supplements. These sketches will remind you what state you are trying to ease or cure (your symptom *energy x*) and what state you are trying to achieve or get back to (*y energy*). Every time you take a pill, look at the sketches and remember both states.

**Health Beliefs**

1. Recall the last time you had the flu[93]. Remember the state the flu forced you into. Describe it in a few words. Find the energy of that flu state. Express it with a hand motion or an energy sketch on a piece of paper.

2. Find the role or part of you this energy is against or that suffers from it. Describe this energy of your usual/normal self. Express it with a hand motion or an energy sketch.

3. What are the beliefs and values of either role or experience? How do they differ from each other? With a friend or in your mind role play both sides of the discussion. On whose side are you usually, and why? What is against one or the other side?

**Cultural Competence**

1. Describe your culture, the land and geography it stems from. Describe how it formed you, how it made you who you are and how it contributed to your beliefs and values—and be proud of it.

2. Examine how your culture defines how you treat yourself, how you engage in the world and how you relate to others.

3. Remember someone's behavior or a past personal behavior that irritated or frustrated you.

4. Express that behavior in a gesture and brief sketch.

5. How is that behavior counter-cultural?

6. Imagine opening up to that behavior or energy expressed in the behavior.

7. Think of it as a cultural diversity issue and one that helps you develop cultural competence.

---

93 You can use any other symptom or "illness" or "malady" to explore your beliefs.

### Positive Deviance

1. Identify an individual, group or program that in your mind has a better solution to a health problem than you have. Maybe it is a solution you had in the past.
2. Describe in detail how you imagine they would handle the problem.
3. Visualize becoming one of their peers and applying their solution (if you think you can't do it, imagine faking it).
4. Describe what stands in the way of embodying that new behavior.

### Earth Dreaming

1. Identify a place on earth in which you feel or felt at home, a sense of ease and centeredness.
2. In your imagination, go there and look around. What makes that place so special?
3. Take some time to enjoy the experience of being in that special place.
4. Impregnate yourself with that place and its surroundings.
5. From that place, give yourself an advice or "teaching."

### Fear of Death[94]

1. Are you thinking about death or are afraid of dying?
2. Is there anything you need to do medically to prevent death?
3. In your imagination, how would you die?
4. Now in your mind, allow yourself to die. Where do you imagine your spirit or soul would go?
5. Follow that process and look back at yourself from that place. What would you want to tell yourself?

---

94 Death can be a powerful ally and teacher. Illness and disease confront us with our possible death. If you think about or are afraid of death this exercise can help you find some detachment and renewed meaning.

### Addictive Tendencies

1. Choose an addictive behavior or tendency.
2. Imagine engaging in this behavior and mindfully notice all aspects of that experience.
3. Notice your self-talk and thoughts, and the state you achieve by engaging in this behavior.
4. What is the benefit of that state?
5. How can you attain that state without the addictive substance or behavior?
6. How does that state compensate for another mind-set or attitude in life?

### Abuse[95]

1. Remember an instance of "abuse," a situation that made you feel one down or "powerless."
2. Who are the players involved in creating that experience?
3. Role play the abuser and the victim.
4. Now imagine how you would react as the victim today, with all the knowledge and faculties you have now.
5. In the role play as the victim, react with your current abilities.
6. How is it different from the initial situation?
7. How can the new you help you handle your illness and relations with your providers?

### Rank Awareness

1. Describe your social, psychological and spiritual rank.
2. What can you do to improve it?

95 Experiences of abuse determine the way we treat ourselves and how much self-compassion we can have towards ourselves.

3. How does your rank affect how you relate to your providers, family and caregivers?
4. Imagine sharing how you feel about your rank with your caregivers and providers.

## *Practical Tools and Exercises for Providers and Caregivers*

### The "Difficult" Client or Patient

1. What makes the "difficult" client so difficult?
2. Are there any cultural diversity issues? If yes, imagine mentioning them in your next encounter.
3. Are there any rank issues? Compare your rank with the client's rank. What are the differences?
4. Imagine talking about your and the client's rank in your next visit.
5. Express the client's difficult energy in a gesture and quick sketch.
6. How can that energy teach you how to relate to your client and understand her better?
7. How can you support your client to use her "difficult" energy more consciously?

### Rank Awareness

1. Think about your social, psychological, spiritual and contextual[96] rank. What gives you more power than your client or patient?
2. Talk about your rank with your client. Let him know that you are aware of the rank imbalance.

---

96 Certain contexts and roles can give you rank even though you might feel you have less rank because of social circumstances.

3. Talk with your client about ways he can maintain some sense of control.

## Caregiver Dynamics

In care teams and family systems, individuals get polarized into specific roles. For the person who is sick and whom you are taking care of, you are constituting a field. In this field, frequent roles are the one who is standing for comfort care; the one who is for total or maximized care; and the one who is for more awareness, sharing of feelings and processing relationships. As a provider or a participant in the field, consider mentioning the various roles and sides. If you feel something you might think of saying, play out the whole field and the different sides. Share your feelings, imagine how someone or the patient might react to them and share that feeling, too. You can do this even when the patient is in a non-responsive or non-verbal state of consciousness[97].

1. What is your role and function in the care team?

2. What value and attitude are you representing? Are you for comfort and pain relief? Are you for the maximum care possible? Are you for sharing feelings and processing relationships?

3. Imagine taking your side and mentioning the other sides or roles, as well.

## Relating to the Patient's Symptom

1. Besides gathering facts and information, take time to listen to the patient's subjective experience of her symptom. Ask her to express the energy of her experience in a gesture.

2. Ask your patient about night dreams.

3. Talk about small health and big health, the need for restoring health and for leading a meaningful life.

4. Think about big health and explore with the patient how she can integrate her process in a meaningful way.

97 For more information about communicating with "comatose" patients, see: Pierre Morin & Gary Reiss, *Inside Coma: A New View of Awareness, Healing and Hope* (Santa Barbara, CA: Praeger, 2010).

5. Talk about beliefs and hopes.

6. Talk about your relationship and ways to improve the placebo effect and prevent nocebo side effects.

7. Talk about trust, the need for defensive medicine and assurance and the possibility of uncertainty.

## Burnout

1. Sit back and relax and notice how it feels to be you right now.

2. If you are feeling burned out, tired, depressed or hopeless, explore the experience with curiosity. If you don't feel burned out right now, remember a time when you felt overwhelmed, fatigued, distressed or numbed out.

3. How does that experience feel emotionally, mentally and in your body? Is it lethargy, "brain freeze," heaviness, emptiness, anxiety panic or something else? Uncover that experience with an open mind.

4. Breathe into it and let it engulf you. Give it space and let it move you at its own pace and timing. Become the burnout experience.

5. Explore its way of relating, living, doctoring, helping. Discover its energetic quality. If you want, you can draw a quick energy sketch that captures the essential quality that burnout has for you.

6. Next, ask yourself who in you needs this burnout medicine. Who needs burnout? What part of you is the experience of burnout meant for?

7. Let both parts speak and have a dialogue about their values and motivations.

## Reconnect With Your Initial Vision[98]

1. What motivated you to become a doctor, nurse, therapist, or caregiver?

2. Remember your calling and the vision you had when you started.

3. Describe what currently stands in the way. What disturbs your calling today?

4. In your mind, take a step back and find a more detached place, such as a place on earth that makes you feel at home in yourself.

5. From that vantage point, look back at yourself, your calling and your challenges and examine if that new perspective gives you some answers.

6. Make some notes to remember your insights.

## Defensive Medicine

Here are some questions to consider when suggesting tests or treatments:

1. Is this test or treatment really necessary, and how much are you motivated by fear of overseeing something or making a mistake?

2. Did your patient have this test or treatment previously?

3. If so, what is the indication for repeating it? Is the result of a repeated test likely to be substantively different from the last result?

4. What are the nocebo effects of the treatment or test? How much do you share about the possible side effects and/or the possible false positive results?

5. How can you improve your relationship with the patient, the trust and the placebo effect?

---

98 This is also a good exercise to do with a team. To find the team's sense of home, ask participants where they would want to go on vacation.

6. What are alternative tests or treatments? Who can you refer your patient to for complementary treatments?
7. How much do your interventions cost your patient, and how can you reduce unnecessary costs?

## Conducting Open Forums[99]

1. Identify the main issue you want the community to address. Name the secondary issues[100] that are connected to the main issue.
2. Be clear about your personal goals. Make them explicit. Think about how your goals intersect with the goals of the community. Who in the community might be against your goals?
3. Identify roles and people from the different sides of the issue.
4. Conduct an imaginary open forum with your helping team or in your mind and explore the different viewpoints. How do they represent aspects of yourself or your team?
5. Think about current ways the community is dealing with the issue at hand. Network and collaborate with other people and programs.
6. Speak with elders of the community about the issue you want to address. Get their input and invite them to the forum101.
7. Carefully choose a location and time that works for the community, and create an invitation.

---

99 For more details about open forums, see Arnold Mindell, *The Deep Democracy of Open Forums* (Charlottesville, VA: Hampton Roads Publishing, 2002).

100 Every issue is also an umbrella covering secondary issues; all issues are entangled with other issues (i.e., homelessness connects with economic, class and race issues, as well as issues of relationship with the police and the mental health field).

101 A colleague of mine planned a forum on homophobia and racism. He experienced some backlash and resistance from the local anti-racism community, which forced him to postpone the forum. After integrating their feedback, he was able to conduct a series of successful forums on this very charged topic.

8. Identify co-facilitators that somehow embody the issue being discussed.
9. Choose and invite speakers from the polarized positions. Ask three to four people to speak briefly about the issue from their point of view.
10. At the beginning of the forum, briefly introduce yourself and your team (don't take up too much airtime).
11. Acknowledge any factor that could contribute to marginalizing some participants (i.e., language, communication style, rank, health, etc.).
12. Acknowledge the pain and suffering the issue might elicit in some participants.
13. Invite the identified speakers to initiate the discussion.
14. Frame the ensuing discussion in terms of momentary group atmospheres, roles that are explicitly represented and roles that are missing or talked about. Remember: everyone has all roles inside.
15. If the discussion gets heated, help participants slow down and speak one at a time. Remind yourself and the group that even when very one-sided, a part of you might be able to hear the other side.
16. Close the discussion with framing what has been discussed and what the group has achieved. Suggest the group continue the discussion in small groups and come up with action steps.

## APPENDIX III

# *Definitions*

Democracy: From the Greek "demos," or "common people," and "kratos," or "rule, strength." Democracy implies that common people take responsibility for their own ruling.

Deep democracy: Developed by Arny Mindell in 1988, the term first appeared in *Leader as Martial Artist* (Mindell 1992). "Deep Democracy is the experience of a process of flow in which all actors on the stage are needed to create the play that is being watched."(16) Deep democracy is an attitude that focuses on the awareness and inclusion of diversity, of all the voices— those that are central and marginal, mainstream and unconventional, constructive and disruptive, beneficial and "detrimental" or unfavorable. This type of awareness is both external and internal, including other people, conflicts and social dynamics, as well as internalized representations of these voices and roles.

Disability: An umbrella term and a complex phenomenon, reflecting an interaction between features of a person and features of the society in which he or she lives. Disability refers to impairments or problems in body function and/or structure, activity limitations or the difficulty of executing a task and restrictions of a person's involvement in certain life situations. A disability may be physical, cognitive, mental, sensory, emotional, and developmental or some combination of these. A disability may be present from birth or occur during a person's lifetime. Disability designations justify community support via entitlement benefits (i.e., social security). Disability is at the crossroads between the right for protection, social inclusion and equal opportunities and the "moral" responsibility to be self-sufficient and a productive member of society. It is between the role of the individual and the role of the collective.

Disability rights advocates see the struggles "disabled" people face as a diversity issue. Disabilities are challenges and not just limitations.

Instead, "disabled" people have different abilities that play important roles within our communities and work environments. Eunice Kennedy Shriver, founder of the Special Olympics, taught the world that everyone can learn from people with disabilities.

Disease: Derives from the old French word "desaise" or "lack, want; discomfort, distress; trouble, misfortune; disease, sickness." It comes from "des" or "dis," which means "without, away" and "aise" or "ease" in the sense of "comfort, pleasure, and well-being."

Georges Canguilhem (1989): Disease is a positive innovative experience and not just a fact of decrease or increase. Disease is not a variation on the dimension of health; it is a new dimension of life. Disease is the reduction in one's ability to be normative, to create new norms and adapt to life's challenges. As we age, this becomes part of a normal process.

Mainstream Western medicine: "Diseases are internal states that depress a functional ability below species-typical levels."(Boorse 1977) Diseases are objective and real states or conditions of a person.

Diseases are the categories that practitioners create to explain the causes, the course of a particular process and the prognosis or outcome of that process. They are theories that organize illness experiences into a framework that give practitioners and ill people some orientation and coherence. Diseases are what practitioners have been trained to see through their individual theoretical lenses. Diseases are objective entities void of subjective experiences and outside the social world of the afflicted person. They are the problem from the practitioners' perspective. Like diseases, disorders are a derangement or abnormality of physical or mental functions Injuries are wounds or traumas. The term injury is usually applied to a damage inflicted on the body by an external force.

Disorder: In contrast to disease, which is an abnormal condition affecting the body or mind with an identifiable cause, disorders are disturbances or abnormalities of physical or mental function for which the causes are less certain and left open. The term disorder is often considered more value-neutral and less stigmatizing than the terms disease or illness, and therefore is the preferred terminology in some circumstances. In mental health, the term mental disorder is used as a way of acknowledging the complex interaction of biological, social, and psychological factors in psychiatric conditions.

Health: Derives from the root Old German word "heilag" or "whole, holy." To heal therefore means "to make whole" and healing consists in restoring wholeness. Healing and health are related to the concept of wholeness.

Aaron Antonovsky (1996): Health is "the state of that system we call human organism, which manifests a given level of order."(172) We are healthy despite the ongoing onslaught of potential sickening processes. Entropy and disorder or the movement toward the disease end of the scale is normal and natural. Individuals and communities have salutogenic[102] abilities that keep them resilient.

Big health: Diseases and symptoms are a facet of wholeness. They are fishhooks for developing awareness and meaning. Change and Process are healing and vice versa; healing encompasses change and Process.

Community health: A field of public health. It is a discipline that concerns itself with the study and improvement of the health characteristics of communities. While the term community can be broadly defined, community health tends to focus on geographical areas rather than people with shared characteristics.

René Dubos (1960): Health is a "relatively trouble-free state devoid of suffering."

Global health: Optimal wellness that transcends national boundaries and is best addressed by cooperative solutions. Justice, redemption and restoration are important, and we need to process the roles of abuser, perpetrator, competitor and privileged. They are here to teach us.

Global warming is considered by some to be the largest global health threat of the 21st century.

Harvard Program in Refugee Trauma (HPRT) (Capoor 2001): "Health is a personal and social state of balance and well-being in which people

102 The term describes a medical approach that focuses on factors that support human health and well-being, rather than on factors that cause disease.

feel strong, active, wise and worth-while; where their diverse capacities and rhythms are valued; where they may decide and choose, express themselves, and move freely."

Injury model of health and disease: We are not sick or bad but injured, which takes the moral aspect of disease away. What's wrong with you changes into: What happened to you? Too much or too little of something (i.e., too much force or speed, too little emotional support etc.) can lead to physical, emotional and social injuries. An injury model implies the possibility of recovery and hope.

Mainstream Western medicine: "Absence of or freedom from disease." Statistical normality of biological functions (i.e., the ability to perform all typical physiological functions with at least typical efficiency). An objective and real state or condition of a person.

Arnold Mindell: Health is a somatic feeling connection to your deepest self, which is the maker of dreams and the inner compass pointing to the next step.

Process oriented definition: Health is a consensus reality concept of an idealized state of well-being. Without disease, there is no health. Health is an experience of well-being in contrast to ill-health, pain or suffering but it doesn't exist without pain, suffering and ill-health. Health and ill-health are subjective experiences and are part of a larger dreaming journey, part of a path toward individuation and development for the individual and community. They are part of our own inner and outer diversity. From a dreaming level, health and ill-health are energies, life qualities that cross our path. They inform us about our inner and outer diversity.

Health in itself can be a stressor by creating an unachievable expectation. Mainstream beliefs about health that exclude the symptom experience help co-create and solidify disease experiences. Thinking about health distracts you from the diversity experience expressed in "diseases." The collective thinking that something is wrong is part of the problem.

The health of the community is based on the deep democracy awareness of all the roles, diversity issues and challenges present in a community. Community-based health leadership is the ability to see yourself in all the different roles, which allows you to relate to everyone, invite their views and voices and facilitate from a position of eldership. This is different from advocacy, where you lead from a specific polarized position or role.

Small health: The "veterinary" medicine or consensus reality aspects of one's body. What can be restored through mechanical, biochemical or physiological interventions and treatments. It includes both linear mono-causal and non-linear and complex adaptive processes. Sickness is troublesome, painful, disturbing and bad and needs to be fought against and corrected.

Social determinants of health: Are the economic and social conditions—and their distribution among the population—that influence individual and group differences in health status. They are risk factors found in one's living and working conditions (such as the distribution of income, wealth, influence and power), rather than individual factors (such as behavioral risk factors or genetics) that influence the risk for a disease, or vulnerability to disease or injury[103].

Piet van Spijk (2011): "Health is the ability to lead a meaningful life."

Public health: Is the science and art of protecting and improving the health of communities through education, promotion of healthy lifestyles and research for disease and injury prevention. Public health helps improve the health and well-being of people in local communities and around the globe. Public health works to prevent health problems before they occur.

Total health: A concept pioneered by Kaiser Permanente's cofounder, Sidney R. Garfield, MD. It holds that people need quality medical care and much more to be healthy. For their physical, emotional and spiritual well-being, people need healthy environments where they live, work, play, and relax—in schools, playgrounds, offices and factories, neighborhoods, parks, urban streets and rural byways. This concept is about healthy people, healthy environments and healthy communities.

There's a movement afoot to build more sustainable, livable, healthy communities. It is growing in momentum and collective will, despite

103 http://en.wikipedia.org/wiki/Social_determinants_of_health

what many feel are overwhelming statistics showing the rise of obesity and chronic disease in this country. It is a movement being led by people serving across disciplinary fields and political perspectives—community leaders, health activists, philanthropic organizations and government agencies—all seeking the goal of thriving, healthy communities.

WHO (1946): "Health is a state of complete physical, mental, and social well-being and not merely the absence of disease or infirmity."

<u>Illness:</u> Describes the human experience of symptoms and their associated suffering. It refers to how the sick person, the family and the larger social environment perceive, live with and respond to symptoms. It includes categorizing and assigning meaning to the symptoms. Illness problems are the specific difficulties that symptoms create in our lives. Illness problems and experiences are embedded in a cultural context that "dictates" normal and abnormal ways of being ill.

<u>Medical Condition:</u> Is a broad term that includes all diseases and disorders. Like disorder, it is considered more value-neutral and less stigmatizing. Diagnostic manuals and some insurances use medical condition to differentiate physical diseases, illnesses and injuries from mental disorders and psychiatric illnesses.

<u>Medical Diagnosis:</u> Refers to the process of identifying the nature and cause of a possible disease, disorder or symptom with the goal of mitigating the problem and finding a treatment or cure. A clinician uses several sources of data (medical history, physical examination, tests) and puts the pieces of the puzzle together to make a diagnostic impression.

Process view: A diagnosis substitutes a name for a process. What was previously a fluid and dynamic experiential Process becomes a fixed state with predetermined notions about the causes, solutions and future evolution of the process (i.e., prognosis). Diagnoses are helpful in terms of small health and can be detrimental in terms of big health.

<u>Medicine:</u> From the Latin word "ars medicina," "the medical art," and from the Latin verb "mederi," "to heal, give medical attention to, cure." It includes the early Indo-European root "med," "to measure, limit, consider, advise," and is related to the Greek verbs "medomai," "be

mindful of," "medein," "to rule" and the Latin verb "meditari," "think or reflect on, consider."

Medicine designates the profession of healing and involves the economics of health care and doctor-patient relationship. It describes the practice of controlling the disease process and caring for the receiver of services and his or her illness experience. Medicine incorporates the social dynamics in which healing practices are embedded, as well as the diversity of therapeutic professions that are part of the health care systems (chiropractic, osteopathy, naturopathy, nurses, social workers, counselors and psychologists, physical and occupational therapists, dentists, translators, technicians, etc.). The sciences of medicine are the sources of knowledge that inform the various practices. They include biology, psychology, sociology, philosophy, anthropology, history and ethics. New trends in medicine integrate behavioral, dental and medical sciences under one holistic medical home umbrella that aims at improving care through better collaboration and coordination and reducing costs by being more efficient and avoiding redundant and unnecessary procedures and services.

Evidence-based medicine: Is "the conscientious, explicit and judicious use of current best evidence in making decisions about the care of the individual patient. It means integrating individual clinical expertise with the best available external clinical evidence from systematic research" (Sackett 1996). It seeks to assess the strength of the evidence of risks and benefits of treatments (including lack of treatment) and diagnostic tests. This helps clinicians predict whether a treatment will do more good than harm. It is an attempt to standardize medical processes, make them more efficient and cost effective and get the best possible outcomes or results.

Critics say that the evidence is based on quantitative randomized controlled trials (the gold standard of clinical research), which have several limitations. They marginalize individual differences, clinical experience and the doctor-patient relationship and are not representative of certain segments of the population (i.e., racial minorities and people with co-morbid diseases).

Morality: Derived from the Latin moralitas, or "manner, character, proper behavior." It is the differentiation of intentions, decisions and actions between those that are "good" (or right) and those that are "bad" (or wrong). Ethics is the philosophy of morality, and moral code is a system of morality (according to a particular philosophy, religion, culture, etc.). To live a moral life is to live following a moral code. Morality may also be specifically synonymous with "goodness" or "rightness." An example of a moral code is the Golden Rule, which states that "one should treat others as one would like others to treat oneself."

Nocebo: The negative side effects observed while giving a placebo.

Normal: From the Latin "normalis," which originally denoted "standing at a right angle or made according to a carpenter's T- square." This led to the meaning "in conformity with rule."

The philosopher Ian Hacking (1990) postulates that the idea of normal currently contains both the meaning of an existing average and a state of perfection toward which individuals or societies can strive. Normal includes not only the concept of an objective average but also the notion of good health. Diseases have become part of a moral dispute about the boundaries of normal and abnormal.

Biochemistry: Normal in biochemistry means according to the reference value. Biological characteristics that are representative of healthy humans and presented in a manner that can be replicated by all laboratories. It is defined statistically from populations of healthy subjects.

Normality in community: In statistics, a normal distribution describes a population whose characteristics center around the average or norm. Normal is also used to describe when someone's behavior conforms to the most common behavior in society (known as conforming to the norm). Definitions of normality vary by person, time, place and situation—they shift along with changing societal standards and norms. Normal behavior is often only recognized in contrast to abnormality. In its simplest form, normality is seen as good, while abnormality is seen as bad. When someone is seen as "normal" or "not normal," this can have social ramifications, such as being included, excluded or stigmatized by the larger society.[104]

Georges Canguilhem (1989): Normal is that which bends neither to the right nor left, hence that which remains in a happy medium. Normal is that which is such that it ought to be, that which constitutes either the average or standard of a measurable characteristic. An individual (living being) is normal in any given environment insofar as it is the morphological and functional solution found by life as a response to the demands of the environment. Normal is always in relationship to the environment.

Normality in medicine and psychiatry: Applying normality to clinical situations depends on the field and situation a practitioner is in. In the broadest sense, clinical normality is the idea of uniformity of physical and psychological functioning across individuals. Normality and abnormality can be characterized statistically. Statistical normality (see below) is usually defined it in terms of a normal distribution curve. As a relative concept, is intrinsically involved with contextual elements. As a result, clinical disorder classification has particular challenges in discretely diagnosing "normal" constitutions from true disorders. The WHO developed a medical classification list called the International Statistical Classification of Diseases and Related Health Problems. The ICD-10 is in its tenth revision. It codes for diseases, signs and symptoms, abnormal findings, complaints, social circumstances and external causes of injury or diseases. These classifications are created through majority votes from expert panels that are not inclusive of the existing diversity in medical opinions.

Many other efforts have been undertaken to standardize the language, terminology and outcomes of clinical practices. The Nursing Outcomes Classification (NOC) is a system that describes patient outcomes sensitive to nursing intervention. The NOC is evaluates the effects of nursing care as a part of the nursing process. It contains 330 outcomes, each with a label, definition and a set of indicators and measures to determine achievement of the nursing outcome.

Systemized nomenclatures of pathology and clinical terms (SNOP, SNOMED and SNOMED CT) are creating systematically organized,

104 http://en.wikipedia.org/wiki/Normality_(behavior)

computerized collections of medical codes, terms, synonyms and definitions covering diseases, findings, procedures, microorganisms, substances, etc. They allow a consistent way to index, store, retrieve and aggregate clinical data across specialties and sites of care. They also help organize the content of medical records, reducing variability in the way data is captured, encoded and used for clinical care of patients and research. The Medical Subject Headings (MeSH®) thesaurus is a controlled vocabulary produced by the National Library of Medicine and used for indexing, cataloging and searching for biomedical and health-related information and documents.

Some thinkers and researchers challenge concepts of normality that are based on averages. They argue for a re-orientation toward excellent physical and mental health, which draws from exceptional people. Normality, which is derived from the average of a reference group, derives standards of good mental and physical health that stay suboptimal.

Normative normality: That which is such as it should be (value norm).

Statistical normality: That which occurs in the majority of cases or which constitutes either the mean or the mode of a measurable characteristic (frequency norm). The average or the norm commonly accounts for 95.45 percent of all the data. The remaining 4.55 percent lie split outside of two standard deviations from the mean. Thus, any variable case that lies outside of two deviations from the mean would be considered abnormal.

Pathology: The word pathology is from the ancient Greek pathos, which means "feeling, suffering," and -logia, "the study of." It is now used for the precise study and diagnosis of disease. Medically speaking, pathologies are synonymous with diseases. To pathologize refers to the process of defining a condition or behavior as pathological (e.g., pathological gambling). Pathology is also a medical specialty which focuses on studying diseases and cause of death through examination of organs, tissues, bodily fluids and whole bodies (autopsies).

Social pathology: Is the study of social problems or factors that contribute to social disorganization. These include poverty, homelessness, substance abuse, violence, abuse of women and children, crime, terrorism, corruption, criminality, discrimination, isolation, stigmatization and human rights violations. Definitions of social pathology are particular to specific times and cultural contexts. They reflect the dominant moral concerns of the era. Social stability and order reflect dominant social values and are considered natural and normal by the mainstream. Social diversity and change are perceived as threats to the status quo and relegated to the sphere of the abnormal and dangerous. Marginalized and disadvantaged people who are excluded from the mainstream, such as single mothers, nonwhites and non-heterosexuals, are in danger of being stigmatized and pathologized as socially deviant.

Placebo: From the Latin verb "placer," or "to please." The medical sense is first recorded in 1785: "a medicine given more to please than to benefit the patient."[105]

Power: Derived from the Old French verb "povoir," or Latin "potere," "to be able." One of the most cited definitions comes from Max Weber (1978), who defined power as the possibility of imposing one's own will on the behavior of others even against opposition. His definition stresses the coercive aspect of power. Hannah Arendt (1970), on the other hand, differentiates between an individual and a collective dimension of power and transcends the one-sided coercive reference of the word. For the individual dimension of power, she reserves the term "strength." For her, power is intrinsically an attribute related to the collective.

> Power corresponds to the human ability not just to act but to act in concert. Power is never the property of an individual; it belongs to a group and remains in existence only so long as the group keeps together. When we say of somebody that he is 'in power' we actually refer to his being empowered by a certain number of people to act in their name. (59)

Process: Derived from the Latin verb "procedure," which means "to move forward." This reflects the dynamic aspect of the concept. In phi-

105 http://www.etymonline.com/?search=placebo

losophy, Process designates "a succession of phenomena presenting a certain unity or that are reproduced with certain regularity."[106]

Arnold Mindell: Process is the dynamic and directed movement in space and time, the journey that our bodies lead us through and the story that they narrate. Health is not a state but a Process and the tales and discoveries that come with health and illness are not only fateful but part of our meaningful path through life's developmental process.

Rank: The position of a person, place, thing or idea in relation to others based on a shared property such as physical location, population or quality. It is derived from the Frankish word "hring," or "ring," and the Old French words "reng, rang, ranc," or "line, row, rank." It characterizes the stratification and distribution of power and privileges within a community and determines access to privileges.

Sickness: The mainstream understanding across a large group of people of a disease or illness process in relation to economic, political and social forces. Sickness is what justifies the support of entitlement programs such as health care insurance for the poor and elderly and social security disability. When we talk of the relationship of a disease process with poverty or other social determinants we are invoking disease and illness as sickness. Sickness is what informs the public health domain and embeds the illness experience in a social field. This includes marginalization and other social dynamics of rank and privilege, such as poverty, lack of access to education and safe housing, racism, sexism, homophobia, etc.

Psychological sickness can be associated with badness. Something is wrong and possibly caused by wrong and bad behaviors.

Social Capital: The sum of social relations and networks that have productive benefits. Social capital is about the value of social networks, bonding similar people and building bridges between diverse people, with norms of reciprocity. Social capital is "the goodwill available to individuals or groups. Its source lies in the structure and content of the

106 http://www.encyclopedia.com/topic/Process.aspx

actor's social relations. Its effects flow from the information, influence and solidarity it makes available to the actor."[107]

Status: Derived from the Latin "statum," or "standing." In a narrow sense, status refers to a person's legal or professional standing within a group. Psychologically, it also stands for one's value and importance in the eyes of others.

Symptom: Stems from the Greek words "sympiptein," "to befall," and "symptomatos," "a happening, accident, disease." Symptoms describe the manifestations of a disease. They carry cultural significance and are identified in a consensus process between practitioners and individuals or communities. Symptoms are dependent on the contextual, culturally agreed-upon knowledge about the body, its functions and "pathologies." Some symptoms carry differing value in the eyes of practitioners and the individual experiencing them. This can lead to misunderstandings, conflict and lack of compliance with the practitioner's recommendations.

Symptoms in our culture mean something "bad." The word itself means accidental happening, neither good nor bad. The judgment of their value need not be moral, and as accidental happenings they belong in the realm of destiny and not medicine alone. If the symptom is not only bad, we can open up to its image or information. This allows us to open our eyes to the intention in a symptom. If symptoms lose their moral connotation as wrong, we can approach them with less anxiety and simply as a phenomenon or experience.

107 Paul S. Adler and Seok-Woo Kwon. Social Capital: Prospects for a New Concept. *The Academy of Management Review* 27: 17-40, (2002, 23).

# BIBLIOGRAPHY


Ader, R. and N. Cohen. 1984. "Behaviorally conditioned immunosuppression and murine systemic lupus erythematosus." *Science*, 226: 70-72.

Antonovsky, Aaron. 1979. *Health, Stress and Coping: New Perspectives on Mental and Physical Well-Being*. San Francisco, CA: Jossey-Bass.

Arendt, Hannah. 1986. *On Violence*. Reprinted in St. Lukes (Ed.), *Power*. New York, NY: New York University Press.

Benedetti, Fabrizio et al. 2006. "The Biochemical and Neuroendocrine Bases of the Hyperalgesic Nocebo Effect." *The Journal of Neuroscience*, 26(46).

Bergson, Henri. 1911. *Creative Evolution*. New York, NY: H. Holt and company.

Boorse, Christopher. 1977. Health as a Theoretical Concept. *Philosophy of Sciences*, Vol. 44, No 4: 542-573.

Brown, Brené. 2010. *The Gifts of Imperfection*. Center City, MN: Hazelden.

Brunet, Alain et al. 2008. "Effect of post-retrieval propranolol on psychophysiologic responding during subsequent script-driven traumatic imagery in post-traumatic stress disorder." *Journal of Psychiatric Research*, 42 (6): 503-6.

Bush, Haydn. 2013. Caring for the Costliest. *Hospital and Health Networks*. http://www.hhnmag.com/hhnmag/jsp/articledisplay.jsp?dcrpath=HHNMAG/Article/data/11NOV2012/1112HHN_Coverstory&domain=HHNMAG. Accessed 22 September 2013.

Canguilhem, Georges. 1989. *The Normal and the Pathological*. Brooklyn, New York, NY: Urzone Inc.

Capoor, I. 2001. Power of definition in global health. Fulbright new century scholars program. October 29 to November 11, Bellagio. http://www.cies.org/ncs/2001_2002/download/meetingreport_bellagio.pdf. Accessed 22 September, 2013.

Chida, Y. et al. 2008. "Do stress-related psychosocial factors contribute to cancer incidence and survival?" *Nature Clinical Practice: Oncology*, 5(8):466–75.

Colton, Craig W. and Ronald W. Manderscheid. 2006. "Congruencies in increased mortality rates, years of potential life lost, and causes of death among public mental health clients in eight states." *Preventing Chronic Disease*, Vol. 3, No 2.

Cousin, Norman. 1979. *The Anatomy of an Illness*. New York, NY: W.W. Norton and Company Inc.

Crawford, R. 1980. "Healthism and the medicalisation of everyday life." *Int J Health Serv*, 10: 365–88.

Cross, T. et al. 1989. *Towards A Culturally Competent System of Care Volume I*. Washington, D.C.: Georgetown University Child Development Center, CASSP Technical Assistance Center. http://www.mhsoac.ca.gov/meetings/docs/Meetings/2010/June/CLCC_Tab_4_Towards_Culturally_Competent_System.pdf. Accessed 22 September, 2013.

Dossey, Larry. 1987. *The importance of Whitehead's Philosophy to Modern Medicine*. In: M.P. Ford (Ed.), A Process Theory of Medicine. Lewiston, NY: Edwin Mellen Press.

Dossey, Larry. 1999. "Healing and Modern Physics: Exploring Consciousness and the Small-Is-Beautiful Assumption." *Alternative Therapies*, Vol 5, No. 4.

Dubos, René. 1960. *The Mirage of Health*. London: Allen and Unwin.

Dubos, René. 1968. *Man, Medicine, and Environment*. New York, NY: Frederick A. Praeger.

Eagleman, David. 2011. *Incognito: The secret lives of the brain*. New York, NY: Pantheon Books.

Einstein, Albert. 1955. *The Meaning of Relativity*. Princeton, NJ: Princeton University Press.

Fain, Jean. 2011. *The Self-Compassion Diet*. Boulder, CO: Sounds True.

Frankl, Viktor. 2006. *Man's Search for Meaning*. Boston, MA: Beacon Press.

Finch, David. 2012. *The Journal of Best Practices*. New York, NY: Scribner.

Gawande, Atul. 2011. "The Hot Spotters." *The New Yorker*. January 24, 2011.

Gendlin, Eugene. 1997. *Experiencing and the Creation of Meaning: A Philosophical and Psychological Approach to the Subjective.* Evanston, IL: Northwestern University Press.

Goodbead, Joe. 2009. *Living on the edge: the mythical, spiritual, and philosophical roots of social marginality.* New York, NY: Nova Science Publishers.

Guggenbühl-Craig, Adolf. 1999. *The Archetype of the Invalid and the Limits of Healing* in *The Emptied Soul*, ed. Adolf Guggenbühl-Craig and James Hillman. Woodstock, CT: Spring Publications.

Hall, Kathryn T. et al. 2012. "Catechol-O-Methyltransferase val-158met Polymorphism Predicts Placebo Effect in Irritable Bowel Syndrome." http://www.plosone.org/article/info%3Adoi%2F10.1371%2Fjournal.pone.0048135. Accessed 22 September, 2013.

Halpern, Susan P. 2004. *The Etiquette of Illness*. New York, NY: Bloomsbury.

Harringtone, Ane. 1999. *Reenchanted Science –Holism in German Culture from Wilhelm II to Hitler.* Princeton, NJ: Paperbacks.

Hertzman, C. 1999. "The Biological Embedding of Early Experience and Its Effects on Health in Adulthood." *Annals of the New York Academy of Sciences* 896: 85-95.

Heschel, Abraham Joshua. 1954. *Man's Quest for God.* New York, NY: Charles Scribner's Sons.

Heschel, Abraham Joshua. 1961. *To Grow in Wisdom.* Paper presented to the White House Conference on Aging, Washington, D.C., January 9, 1961.

Ji, J. et al. 2012. "Incidence of Cancer in Patients with Schizophrenia and Their First-Degree Relatives: A Population-Based Study in Sweden." *Schizophr Bull.*

Jung, Carl. 1961. *Memories, Dreams, Reflections.* New York, NY: Random House.

Kalat, J.W. 2001. *Biological Psychology.* Belmont, CA: Wadsworth Thomson Learning.

Kano, Noriaki et al. 1984. "Attractive quality and must-be quality." *The Journal of the Japanese Society for Quality Control*, 39-48.

Kennedy, E. 1989. *A Cultural History of the French Revolution.* New Haven, CT: Yale University Press.

Kleinman, A. and D. Seeman. 2000. *Personal Experience of Illness*. In G.A. Albrecht, R. Fitzpatrick, & S.C. Scrimshaw (Eds.). The Handbook of Social Studies in health And Medicine. London: Sage Publications.

Kohlberg, L. 1976. *Moral stages and moralization: The cognitive-developmental approach*. In T. Lickona (Ed.), Moral development and behavior: Theory, research, and social issues (pp.31-53). New York, NY: Holt, Rinehart and Winston.

Lei, T. and S. Cheng. 1987. *A little but special light on the universality of moral judgment development.* Cambridge: Unpublished manuscript, Harvard University.

Levine, Jon D. and Newton C. Gordon, Howard L. Fields. 1978. "The Mechanism of Placebo Analgesia." *The Lancet*, 8091: 654–57.

Lown, Bernhard. 1999. *The Lost Art of Healing: Practicing Compassion in Medicine.* New York, NY: Ballantine Books.

Main, Tom and Adrian Slywotsky. 2012. *The Volume to Value Revolution: Rebuilding the DNA of Health from the Patient In.* http://www.oliverwyman.com/volume-to-value-revolution.htm#.UR0xvKWTwrU. Accessed 13 April, 2013.

Marmot, M.G. and G. Rose, M. Shipley, P.J. Hamilton. 1978. "Employment grade and coronary heart disease in British civil servants." *Journal of Epidemiology and Community Health* 32 (4): 244–249.

Martin, E. 1994. Flexible *Bodies: Tracking Immunity in American Culture from the Days of Polio to the Age of AIDS.* Boston, MA: Beacon Press.

McEwen, B.S. and T. Seeman. 1999. "Protective and Damaging Effects of Mediators of Stress. Elaborating and Testing the Concepts of Allostasis and Allostatic Load." *Annals of the New York Academy of Sciences*, 896: 30-47.

Mindell, Arnold. 1984. *Dreambody.* London: Routledge and Kegan.

Mindell, Arnold. 2000. *The Leader as Martial Artist: An Introduction to Deep Democracy, Techniques and Strategies for Resolving Conflict and Creating COMMUNITY.* Portland, OR: Lao Tse Press.

Mindell, Arnold. 2000. *Quantum Mind, The Edge Between Physics and Psychology.* Portland, OR: Lao Tse Press.

Mindell, Arnold. 2002. *The Deep Democracy of Open Forums.* Charlottesville, VA: Hampton Roads.

Mindell, Arnold. 2004. *The Quantum Mind and Healing.* Charlottesville, VA: Hampton Roads.

Mindell, Arnold. 2010. *ProcessMind: A User's Guide to Connecting with the Mind of God.* Wheaton, IL: Quest Books.

Mindell Arnold. 2013. *The Essence of Process Work—The Tao of Lao Tse.* Winter Class, Process Work Institute, Portland, OR.

Mondaini, Nicola et al. 2007. "Finasteride 5 mg and sexual side effects: how many of these are related to a nocebo phenomenon." *J Sex Med* 4: 1708-1712.

Morin, Pierre and Gary Reiss. 2010. *Inside Coma: A New View of Awareness, Healing, and Hope*. Santa Barbara, CA: Praeger.

Neisser, U. and R. Fivush. 1994. *The remembering self: construction and accuracy in the self-narrative.* New York, NY: Cambridge University Press.

Pelletier, K.R. 1993. *Between Mind and Body: Stress, Emotions, and Health*. In: D. Goleman & J. Gurin (Eds.) Mind Body Medicine. New York, NY: Consumer Reports Books.

Rand, Ayn. 1962. "Introducing Objectivism." *The Objectivist Newsletter* Vol. 1 No. 8.

Sackett, D. 1996. "Evidence-based Medicine - What it is and what it isn't." *British Medical Journal,* 312: 71-72.

Sacks, Jonathan. 2002. *The Dignity of Difference: How to Avoid the Clash of Civilizations.* New York, NY: Continuum International Publishing Group.

Selten, J.P., Cantor-Graae, E. and Kahn, R.S. 2007. "Migration and schizophrenia." *Curr Opin Psychiatry.* 20(2): 111-5.

Shabahangi, Nader Robert. 2010. "The Poetics of Ageing and Dementia." *Journal of Humanistic Psychology,* vol. 50 no. 2: 187-196.

Shapiro, A.K. 1968. "Semantics of the placebo." *Psychiatr Q.* 42 (4): 653–95.

Sheldrake, Rupert. 2009. *Morphic Resonance: The Nature of Formative Causation.* Rochester, VT: Park Street Press.

Schupbach, Max. 2012. Personal communication, October 15.

Sins Invalid. 2013. *http://www.sinsinvalid.org/index.html.* Accessed 13 April, 2013.

Toombs, S.K. 1995. *Sufficient Unto the Day: A Life with Multiple Sclerosis*. In: S.K. Toombs, Barnard, & R.A. Carson (Eds.). Chronic Illness: From Experience to Policy. Bloomington, IN: Indiana University Press.

Tracey, Irene. 2010. "Getting the pain you expect: mechanisms of placebo, nocebo and reappraisal effects in humans." *Nature Medicine* 16: 1277–1283.

Uexküll , Jakob. 1909. *Umwelt und Innenwelt der Tiere.* Berlin, Germany: J. Springer.

United Nation Human Development Report. 2011. http://hdr.undp.org/en/reports/global/hdr2011/. Accessed 13 April, 2013.

Van Spijk, Piet. 2011. *Was ist Gesundheit? Anthropologische Grundlagen der Medizin*. Freiburg, Germany: Verlag Karl Alber.

Voelker, R. 1996. "Nocebos Contribute to a Host of Ills." *Journal of the American Medical Association* 275, no. 5: 345-47.

Weber, Max. 1978. *Economy and Society*. G. Roth and C. Wittich (Eds.) Los Angeles, CA: University of California Press.

Whitehead, Alfred North. 1966. *Modes of Thought.* New York, NY: Macmillan.

Wilper, Andrew P. et al. 2009. "Health Insurance and Mortality in US Adults." Am J Public Health 99 (12): 2289-2295.

World Health Organization. 1946. *Preamble to the Constitution of the World Health Organization as adopted by the International Health Conference, New York, 19-22 June, 1946*; signed on 22 July 1946 by the representatives of 61 States (Official Records of the World Health Organization, no. 2, p. 100) and entered into force on 7 April 1948.

Zultner, R.E. and G.H. Mazur. 2006. *The Kano Model: Recent Developments*. The eighteenth symposium on Quality Function Deployment. http://www.mazur.net/works/Zultner_Mazur_2006_Kano_Recent_Developments.pdf. Accessed 22 September, 2013.

# About the Author

**Pierre Morin**, MD, PhD, is president of the International Association of Process oriented Psychology (IAPOP) and a founding faculty member at the Process Work Institute Graduate School in Portland, OR. He was a clinical director of Switzerland's leading rehabilitation clinic for brain and spinal injuries. After moving to Portland, OR, he studied health psychology and rehabilitation psychology. He currently works as a clinical director and supervisor in an outpatient mental health program and in private practice. Dr. Morin is a co-author of *Inside Coma* and has written numerous articles on mind-body medicine and community health.

## Welcome to DDX

Welcome inside a publication of the Deep Democracy Exchange (DDX), the publishing house of the Deep Democracy Institute.

We produce books, films, music, visual art, and other media that contribute to the research and development of transdisciplinary approaches to both learn from the challenges that we face as a species and as a planet, and overcome them. Although these challenges may seem overwhelming at times, they also serve as catalysts to create new knowledge and further unlikely connections, both in terms of communities as well as in terms of scientific thinking. Along with the growing complexity of our world, we also see a growing interest in finding holistic, all-inclusive perspectives that can address our yearning to understand ourselves as individuals and as part of the whole.

Pierre Morin's book "Health-in-Sickness Sickness-in-Health" fits very well in this perspective. In the tradition started by Arnold Mindells "Dreambody" it is bringing together fields of knowledge such as public health, psychology, neuroscience and systems theory with the importance and potential meaning of our subjective experiences as individuals.

Made in the USA
San Bernardino, CA
26 January 2017